My Attrition

Alan Shope

iUniverse, Inc.
New York   Bloomington

My Attrition

Copyright © 2008 by G. Alan Shope

iUniverse books may be ordered through booksellers or by contacting:

iUniverse
1663 Liberty Drive
Bloomington, IN 47403
www.iuniverse.com
1-800-Authors (1-800-288-4677)

ISBN: 978-0-595-53232-2 (pbk)
ISBN: 978-0-595-63295-4 (ebk)

Printed in the United States of America

iUniverse Rev. Date 2/17/2009

To my mother, Donna Mae Shope (1943–1992).

Or Lifelong Friends, the People We Never Forget.

Contents

My Attrition

He wrote a long, sad letter.
It was his attrition.

Prologue

"If the earth is my real world, then you are my sky at sunset, beautiful, colorful, memorable, never touching the earth and always out of reach."

The nail that holds together the limp, old, faded cabin is a rusty one. The sharp and pointed metal has lived its lifetime in one place, a small wedged hole. Now all that surrounds it begins to fall. The dried timber and worn walls have given way as the roof has become too heavy for those walls to support it. First, on any given winter day, the 150 plus years of time, wind, and weather show themselves.

It begins with a soft, light snowfall. Then more white flakes begin to fall and gather on the old roof. They collect and spread, seeming to call more and more of their friends down to the soft wooden and clay roof. Drifts compile, and the wind starts to blow, forcing more and more flakes onto the roof. They stack and collect. Soon several inches dominate the wooden structure—so much so that the gray and brown faded wood becomes all white with snow. Then a small crack is heard to no one but the air. Then there is another crack, this one larger than the last as it echoes off into the countryside. Seconds later the once-strong roof rattles and shakes.

In the matter of just a few seconds, all that was built over 150 years comes crumbling down inside the four vacant walls. No one is there to see or hear the tragedy that has just taken place. The cabin had long since been evacuated and forgotten, except by the scenery. But time would not win this day; the walls would continue to stand. Months later, maybe years later, the snow that has collected inside the cabin begins to melt. The seasonal, slow rivers of water that build up against the walls and floor work their way to the edge of this small wooden structure. The water collects, and the next year it does the same. The following year more snow means more melted water and even more the year after. Over time the wood at the base of these strong walls begins to wear and splinter. Then, on a soft, windy spring day just enough flowing air catches the bottom post from one of the water-collected walls and shakes it.

The vibration is nothing more than the strength of footsteps that used to walk the paths of this cabin several years earlier, but that's all time needs for another crack to echo across the countryside once more. This one is solo and forces the bottom of the gray-and-black, worn wooden post to snap and the south wall to give way and tumble, returning to the dirt in which it was born. The wooden and clay roof that had collapsed inside the cabin several years earlier heavily pushes the walls outward, and then the complete wall comes crashing down and slides outward, as if to escape down the slightly tilted mountain.

Once again, no one but the birds in a nearby tree heard the devastating collapse, and a doe that was frightened now heads in the opposite direction. Over the next several years the weight of the collapsed wall will eventually take the entire cabin, all four walls giving way to gravity and sliding downward to match the slope of the hillside. Then, some fifty years later, nothing remains but the rotten stack of gray, sun-dried wood. There are no more cracks because the cabin is now at peace. There is no stress from the sidewalls, and gravity has moved on to the next old structure.

The stories and the lives that lived here are all now gone. The proud people who built this home and their proud children who lived in it and their great-grandchildren who had come here are all gone. They too are now a part of this earth, pulled back into the ground like so many other living and nonliving structures before them. Everything that lived here is gone. Even the love from the small nail passes. It is at this time that the smooth south wind blows and whistles through the pile of rotting, bug-infested wood, pushing on the small metal rusted nail that can no longer grasp its home. The weather seems to be taking this cabin apart piece by piece, but it is taking time. That's okay; the weather has plenty of time.

The small, rusty nail slips out of the warm hole and falls to the ground. Not a sound is made—at least not one that will ever be heard by any living creature. The rusty nail has lived up to the responsibility, and it too is now free to return to the earth. It hits the dirt with a small poof and kicks up just enough dirt to cover itself when the tiny cloud settles. The small, metal, rusty nail now too becomes a part of the earth that surrounds it. The cabin is no more. The only vision still seen on this hillside is a small rock garden that has been overcome by large weeds. The garden is made up of hundreds of rocks, large pointed stones that are stacked on top of each other, each rock having its own distinct pattern and shape. Over time some of the dirty rocks have fallen off, but the outline of the stone chapel remains. If undisturbed, it will continue to live on till the end of time itself. Maybe this is why the weather has been so cruel to the old cabin—because the strength that lies in the rocks is a strength that can never be destroyed.

Part 1

When a man has nothing to lose, he has nothing to gain and no incentive to live. He must find a reason to live and never let it go or else he will be haunted by it forever.

The days would flow like water funneling out of the drain, free and unbridled. The months were the pipes that carried it away. The generations were the fields of water left behind. Some would dry up, yet others would find enough moisture to sustain them. But the land was permanent, never giving to the years. The solid green pastures flowed longer than time itself. They were pastures good men would fight to the death to keep but would not possess over time.

The young, desperate fighters and the young, desperate generations would pass over time, giving way to new generations that would occupy the water and land. Yet the green bands of grass that grew would forever withstand the test of time. No matter who tended the fields each year, the grass would always come back with the same beautiful color. It was the constant, reliable earth supplying life and time to the men who occupied it. This was the way of the lords. The land and water belonged to men for a speck of time, and then it would be fought over again. This was the way it was and always would be. This was Stone Chapel, a mountain no man could ever claim, because it belonged to a woman. But her heart would forever belong to a man.

Eve Stone stood at the foot of the flowing hills, tightly grasping an aged piece of paper and a book-flattened sunflower now crumpled in her hand. She wore no jewelry, only an old, rusting piece of woven metal around one

1

finger on her left hand. The homemade ring had not left her hand since it was first placed there many decades earlier.

The woman was overlooking what she had named the Stone Chapel Valley. It was beautiful land, and to her it was more than home. The land was family and the only family she had really known lived here and now in her heart. She had fought many battles in her long life to keep this view. She had been just a young child when she was forced from her home and driven to this place of solitude. It was her grandfather's secret place in the hills, but long after his death it became Eve's home.

She was all that remained from her Stone Chapel family, although to this day she was still hoping to see her true love return. She was now in the final drips of her water, and the drain was very rusty. The pipes continued to drink each and every drop that fell, and it would not be long till the water stopped. She knew this, however: her inner soul could not help but continue to hope for a dream that had long since passed, a dream that had a beginning and middle but no end. That was what she longed for in her final hours.

A soft, clear tear began to build in Eve's heart and continued into her soul. A solo strand of water began in the corner of her faded green left eye. The water crept slowly down the valley that had become her face and across the wrinkles that now appeared as large as eroded canyons covering this once-beautiful English face. The tear rolled around the cheek and fluttered slightly in the harsh wind, as did parts of her solid white hair. Then the tear disappeared into the large green winter blanket that was wrapped around her seemingly tiny shoulders. The blanket neatly covered her entire body but exposed her white ankles and bare white feet as she stood and fought the winter breeze. Her hair was exposed from the top of the blanket and blew in strands around her head while she overlooked the view she had come to love. It was a tear of sadness for all the good times that had long since passed. For every wrinkle on her magnificently well-aged face another tear began to roll. More than just sadness … each of the tears represented a different memory, a different story, a different feeling that had lived in her body all these years. But most of the memories in her life were of one man and his story and a time that made most sense to Eve, yet the world at that time made little sense. That's what made this place so special.

It was the story that she would never forget and one she thought about nearly every day of her life. It was a time of extreme joy and extreme pain. It was a time she would see the man she loved fight for his life and the protection of this special place. It was a time to defend everything and every notion the Stone family held sacred. Eve Stone was now an old woman, but it was time that brought her to this point, and it was time that robbed her of her true love.

In Eve's mind she was still very young and still very much in love with the man who defined the word human; a man who to her was alive somewhere and had never left her heart or her thoughts. He was an American named George Stone, and he was the man who had fought for their love.

THE ATTIC
KANSAS, AMERICA
PRESENT DAY

Through time and space we will never be able to see through the eyes of others. Even the blood that runs through our veins will not supply the courage and the foresight we need to understand what others feel—to see what others see. To each person nature is a different realistic judgment or opinion. Nature is what we make it. This world is what we make of it, but sometimes we can only make it as far as what others see through their eyes. Their thoughts and their lives control the world that surrounds us; their prejudices lay heavy on our shoulders. Thus we are a part of their world and no longer our own.

I feel sometimes that I've been given the eyes of my father. He lived a life about which I know very little. Sixty-three years he spent on this dirt, and I knew almost nothing about him. He was a little boy, a teenager, a war hero, a journalist, a father, and then a memory in my mind … that was his life. His legacy—well, that's a bit different. As far as I knew, I was his only child, the end of the bloodline. I was the end of the name that he had called his own for sixty-three years. But that would change the day I found a small metal box sitting in my attic.

It was a brisk fall day, and I had spent most of the morning cleaning the garage. I was getting used to sneezing from the dirt and dust that were forced upon my nose. The boxes I'd moved that morning had to count in the hundreds. There was no doubt the garage was a huge mess, and I had to get it cleaned out on this short weekend. Snow was on the way, and my car could not take another winter sitting on a frostbit stage in my driveway. I made record time moving the boxes from one side of the garage to the other. I did toss a number of unneeded, unclaimed garage leftovers in the garbage, but for the most part I was making a nice piece of artwork on the south wall. I was taking the dozens and dozens of smaller boxes and stacking them on top of each other, creating a pretty good-looking cardboard wall. Interestingly enough, right as I finished the last box … the wall was full. I was so satisfied with my work that I was motivated to do more. The garage was clean, so I decided to head to the attic.

I grabbed my ladder and maneuvered it to the small door that sat just out of reach along the roof of the garage. I used the long, silver metal ladder to prop the door open and then set the feet of the makeshift metal stairs in place and began my journey upward to the unseen world. I had not been in the attic for several years, and I was not really sure what was up there. Curious of my actions, my older dog, Chip, wandered into the garage to see what I was doing and watched me ascend the ladder. Chip was always on the lookout for food, and whenever there was extra activity, he naturally figured food was involved.

"Sorry, Chip. No food up here!" I muttered.

When I reached the top, I opened the door and a sea of dust came rolling down to my face.

Cough ... my lungs choked.

"Wow," I said softly. "Stay clear, Chip!" He just looked up at me with his solid white-haired face and sneezed in his old dog way and then tried to shake it off. The dust had made its way down to Chip, and he realized it had no smells of passion to it, so he decided to walk over by the back garage door and lie down. He was definitely bored.

I opened the door all the way and progressed into the somewhat sealed tomb that lay above my garage. I could have used a flashlight, but there was just enough light seeping in from the corners of the timbers that I could make my way around. I was delighted to see that there really were not a ton of items up here. *Yep, this job should not take long either!* I thought. Only thing was, some of this stuff looked very fragile. For every turn of my head, I received a different memory of bringing the items to the attic. To the right was a barrel full of all my toys that my mother refused to toss out from my childhood. Every now and then I'd pop that barrel open and bring out my old friends, although I had not done it in several years.

"Wow!" I yelled out. I realized it had been close to fifteen years since the last time I had done that. *Has it been that long since I was up here?* I thought. There were other things that quickly caught my eye, like my grandmother's kitchen lamp. It was very rustic looking now—probably trash for most people, but I remembered how much she loved it, so I never tossed it out. *Maybe now is the time to unload some of this crap,* I thought.

I leaned my head down so as to not hit the cross timber and walked over to the lamp. There was an antique radio and some speakers sitting next to it, along with a dirty, old yellow vase. The vase probably used to be white but over time had faded to a strange color of yellow. It appeared to be as strong as the day it came out of the kiln. This vase wasn't American; it had a kind of French look to it. It was probably my grandmother's as well. There was a box with a ton of eight-track tapes in it. Boy, if this were a garage sale I'd probably turn and walk away; none of this stuff had any real value to it other than the memories my family shared collecting it. I guess that's why I could never throw it away. *Maybe someday long after I'm gone someone will sell it off and another family will take pride in it? The next question—how will I get some of this stuff down my metal stairway to toss out? That is a good question. Maybe I can just move a trashcan over and start dropping it down.* I leaned my head back over the door.

"Hey, Chip, scoot that trash can over here, would ya?"

He didn't reply, and not just because he was now deaf in both ears. I looked back at the boxes, barrels, and lamps and thought, *Let's do this thing!*

I started picking up boxes and carrying them over to the door entrance, always making sure to avoid the clutter. I had turned fifty years old over the summer, and the last thing I needed was to trip, fall, and never see fifty-one. I was only five years from retirement. Fifty-five was going to be the last year that I worked! I was done after that. *Screw sixty-five; even if I make it that far, I would not have many years to enjoy retirement* ... so fifty-five was when I would call it quits. My father only made it to sixty-three and my mother just forty-eight. Colon cancer had taken them both, and two uncles as well. I, no doubt, had the gene as well, and it would take me someday also. For that reason, I had always planned my early retirement.

As I picked up a couple more boxes, the dust and dirt began to fill the red-and-black-checkered flannel sleeves I was wearing. I noticed a small tin box that was stuck between the four others I was trying to carry. The box began to slowly slip and slide through my pressurized grip and was about to fall to the floor. I recognized the box. It was one I remember seeing a couple of times as a child. It belonged to my father, and he used to let me play with it sometimes at Christmas. I always considered the box a tank for my army men, but as I got older, I guess I had just forgotten all about it. It was an old film container that my father owned for years. It was something he truly treasured, and I am not sure what made me forget about it. It wasn't nearly as silver and shiny as it used to be. The dust in the attic had taken care of that.

While staring at the small box, it gave way and let loose of the two larger ones that were holding it together in my grasp. I quickly sent the other boxes crashing to the floor of the attic in an effort to grab the prized possession out of the air, but I failed. The box smashed to the floor of the attic, making a soft crashing sound. The top broke off the hinge, and the bottom bounced off the wooden floor, causing its paper and plastic cargo to shoot out and fill the floor around my feet. As I pulled back from my lackluster effort to catch the box, I noticed that hundreds of small envelopes and letters had collected around my feet. I reached down, picked up a stack of them, and pulled them close. They were handwritten letters that appeared to be from my father, although I could not really remember his handwriting, so I was not sure if he had written them. My interest began to grow as a tiny strand of sunlight made its way through the timbers, across the floor, and onto my hand. Just enough light for me to read the words, *"To my forever love."*

It was at that moment that I began to wonder more about my father's life and what he must have been thinking when he wrote the dozens of stories—this one small metal box held his secret for all these years.

The curiosity of the letters triggered my imagination, and the clean-up work in the attic would have to stop for now. I quickly reached down and picked up all the letters, doing my best to organize them. It was easy to tell the letters had been treated with extreme caution over the years. The creases in them were nearly identical, and while the paper was yellow and a bit crusted, the writing was very easy to see and read. Plastic surrounded each one, along with the metal film canister box that had provided safekeeping for the letters all these years. To think, my father had not read a single word—maybe no one had read a single word—of these mysterious letters or poems in nearly forty years. *That's a long time*, I thought.

My only fear was that my hands, now covered in dirt and dust, would damage the letters. Still, they intrigued me, so I had to open at least one.

I looked around for a chair, and to my delight, there was my mother's pink vanity seat. The vanity had long since been sold, but the chair, like many other former prized objects in my attic, lived out the silent years in darkness.

I reached over and pulled the chair to my rump and then slowly lowered myself down in the seat to make sure the century-old chair could withstand my girth. As I nestled into the chair, it was obvious that it was strong enough to hold my half-century body.

I smiled and looked closely at the letter I had collected in my hands. There had to be at least fifty or sixty small letters surrounding me, and I could tell as I began to sort them that some were newer than others. In fact, some appeared to be quite newer … maybe as many as twenty years newer. There were no dates on the outside of the envelopes that would help me put some kind of timetable on the letters. I was hoping for some clues as I began to read the letters. They appeared to be letters that were written and handed to another person or letters that were written in solace and put away forever. I made this assumption because there did not appear to be any signs of postage on the letters. As I thumbed through the letters, some of them even appeared to have German handwriting on them—at least what I thought was German. I really had no idea.

As I finished my makeshift organization of the letters, newest looking too oldest, I noticed that one of the newer-looking letters appeared to be longer than the others. "So … what the hey?" I asked myself, and opened the newest and longest-looking letter and began to read, hoping to unveil a new form of my father to my memory that had already long since established his legacy to me.

The first letter was titled "My Attrition." I envisioned my father writing it as I began to read it. He wrote a long, sad letter. It was his attrition.

MY ATTRITION

If the earth is my real world, then you are my sky at sunset, beautiful, colorful, memorable, never touching the earth and always out of reach.

Now the only way I can truly love her is to never talk to her again, because I will never see her again. I've waited ... I've tried, but the pain is too great. My life must move forward, and her memory must leave my mind, my body, and my soul, or I will never survive.

I ache ... I really hurt. There is no way to explain the pain that my body feels when it realizes failure, disappointment, and loss. Someone's heart is a terrible thing to lose, but to lose that person is an even greater tragedy. Welcome to my tragedy; it's like a train wreck you see coming from miles ahead but know there is no way to stop it. This is also like the love of someone you can never reach. Faith, destiny, and real life are headed for a three-way collision, but you can do nothing to stop it. You sit back and watch, hoping that somehow the accident will be avoided, but you know in your soul it is inevitable. No matter what you try to do, the circumstances will never change, and the collision that is hard life will eventually happen. So you ride, you watch, and you try to survive.

Honesty is always the best policy, but it's a dish that is sometimes served sour. Not all honesty can be taken in a positive matter. That is why we exaggerate. We don't want to lie, but we try to put down a pillow on which to fall. This is also the place where trust and love really play a huge part in everyday life. Do you understand why I feel this way? Can you help me get through it? These are the questions I ask. These are the answers I search for. Will you open your mind enough to read and understand the pain that I've felt for so many years? Can you help me seal this empty box and mail it away forever? These are the questions I ask you, my lifelong partner.

This is the story, this is the box. Only open it up if you are willing to take this journey with me. Only open it up if you will be a loving partner and understand the feelings that I need to get out. I cannot keep feeling this inside me. I cannot go to the grave without letting every bit of information out. I need people to know who I am and why I care so much. I love people, and I love life. I only hope to make some feel better about who they are. So please understand this is me. Truthful, open, and ready to let out my only secret.

I was never one to believe in love at first sight, but since that day I have become a believer. I know that love at first sight lives, breathes, and will smack you upside the head if you are not careful. But really, when it comes to love, who wants to be careful? There was something about her that hit me hard that day. I knew she would never be mine. I knew that I could never in this world be so lucky as to have her. I did not know why—I just knew—but my heart didn't seem to care. What chemical imbalance did I have that would not allow me to let go of this woman?

I did not know what to think as I spent time in my own personal hell. I had a chance, but I blew it. The door was open, and I just could not get through it. Sometimes true love is a total mystery. Why not me? **Why not me?**

A box of memories can be a great thing, but it can also break your heart. They say, "Never look back; forget the past because there is nothing you can do about it." But I do not believe that. I think there is something you can do about it. I think you can change the future by looking at the past, evaluating the past, and trying to make changes for the better. The question is, who is the better for it? Should we take this life that God gives us and wrap it up in a napkin? Do we take what we are given and say, "Oh well … whatever"? Or is it our responsibility to take this life and be as honest as we can? Should we let those we love know that we love them? Of course! We need to let them know how we feel, when we feel, and just how much we feel. People need to know that they are loved. Our souls need the satisfaction of knowing that their lives have purpose. People need to know that life did not just pass them by. They want to know they made a difference to others and that they were and still are loved.

So when is the proper time to make such an announcement? Here is the question. If I love you, do you want to know it? If your life is set and you are happy or sad, trusted or not, feared or in fear, do you want to hear I love you more than anything I can remember? I am a writer; it is what I do. I sit down and write out my feelings. That is my goal. When I love people, I do what I can to let them know that I am thinking about them. Are my writings wrong? How can they be wrong? People who don't understand this are wrong. People who don't understand that humans desire to be needed are wrong. People who are so full of self-pity and self-greed that they cannot take anyone wanting to express his inner feelings are wrong. I'm not here to change a relationship. God did not put me on this earth to cause problems. He put me here to solve them. Think about that. Love solves problems; it does not create them. Only shallow people create self-absorbed problems.

I will not let society dictate whom I can love or why I love. This is my heart, this is my soul, **this** *is my love. I give it to whom I choose or am chosen by … understand?*

Do we really understand what love is? I do. I know because I have seen both sides of it. There is instant love and there's earned love. These emotions are what we as humans feel. Sometimes greed or fear is a defense mechanism used to try and stop love, but it will never close the door. We are who we are, and we love whom we love.

People say they can find the answers in the stars. Just look up on a clear night and all your questions will be answered. It's true. Sometimes love is like life in the universe. You know it's out there, but it's just so far away that we'll never get together—at least not in this lifetime.

So what do you do about that? Well, you write … then you write some more. You think … then you think some more. You learn to accept, although you don't really want to; you have no choice. It is what it is and that is that. If you swim in the middle of the ocean, sooner or later you will drown unless there is someone there to save you. It is rare that five hundred miles of water in every direction surrounds you and someone can save you. Your best bet is to wash up on a quiet, lonely island, because then you can truly do nothing except wait. That's how I feel. I'm on that island, waiting. Sure, the weather is nice, the scenery is wonderful, and the food is tropical, but I'm alone. No one understands this feeling except for one person, and she is the only one who can save me. Just a few words might get me off this island, but I have not yet had the pleasure of hearing them. A day passes, then weeks, then months, but still no word from her. Does she understand my agony? I know inside that she does. We have a connection that will always keep us on the same page. If she could write, she would. Maybe she thinks I've joined so many others who no longer write or no longer feel? Maybe she thinks I am dead? Maybe she wants to believe that I no longer exist and this is what helps her sleep at night? Maybe this is why she will never attempt to get me off this deserted island, because to her the island sank many years ago? I sit trapped on this island waiting, maybe until the end of my days. How ironic, the only way to truly love her is to never talk to her again. She has a child and a new life. Seeing this face from the past would only upset her balance and sink the ship that I've long hoped would rescue me. I may be on this island indefinitely. There is no other way. If I build my own ship and sail away, build my own ship and find my own way off this island and never return, that could be the answer. The ship would not have the same vision, but it would have the same purpose. Maybe this ship could be bigger and stronger than any man could ever dream he could build. Maybe this ship would be big enough and strong enough to keep the captain from ever looking back at the island paradise he never found. Maybe this new ship was really his paradise and the island was really his hell.

Attrition is a wearing away of the soul. How long will it take to wear mine all the way down to the bone? Will there be anything left if and when I'm released from this island? This will truly test my love for her.

How did we get to this point? How did I lose my true love?

These are the questions that take me to slumber each and every night as I begin to build my new ship.

"Holy crap!" I blurted out. Was this really the writing of my father? What epic story do these letters hold if that was the last one? I had always been told that my father was a journalist of some sort and he really liked to write, but I had no idea the pain he must have felt when he took pen to paper. This long, sad letter was like nothing like I'd ever read before. I could feel the consuming pain from the words he had chosen to use. I quickly understood that I was a part of his new ship—a really small part, but a part. And since I was the last of the bloodline, I guess I was the last crewman on his ship.

My father lived a life long before I was ever born, and it was not a typical life; there is no such thing. These letters proved that. He had love in his heart and love in his mind, and this was long before I was ever born. To me, he was just a man that I called dad. To me, this was his life, and I had never thought about how he got here—to this point, I mean. He died of colon cancer at age sixty-three. His heart must have suffered much more than death several years earlier. Still, I had to hand it to him; he was able to put whatever had troubled him all these years behind him and move on. He married my mother when he was close to thirty-five. While I always thought it just took him a while to find the right woman, the truth was it took that long to get over the last one.

He married my mother and lived a wonderful life. She passed away first, and then it was just the two of us. However, I often questioned if he'd loved someone else after she died. Maybe he sailed that ship back to the island and decided that's where he was going to stay. He truly loved my mother. The two of them lived happily during their time together. They talked, they traveled, and they laughed. They loved, and it was a strong love. I guess he was right about two kinds of love, the instant kind and the kind you earn. He definitely had to earn my mother's love, but she never had to earn his. I only hope they both found what they were looking for in the time they had together.

After that last letter, I was not sure if I was ready to read anymore, but I felt the story was an important one to my father and he probably wanted to share it … so I read on.

KANSAS
LATE *1945*

It was quite possibly the strangest thing George Stone had ever seen in his life, and he had seen a ton of new sights over the last two years. But now he was home, and this is where he was the most bedazzled.

Stone had just recently returned from a war that did not really work out the way he had planned. His assignment was never accomplished, yet he was able to return to Kansas a hero, a former prisoner of war, and a mature adult. For the most part, the war was not kind to George, but for a few months he lived in his own personal heaven. For a couple hundred days George lived the life he had hoped to someday live; only now it was behind him. As Stone looked down at the big rock, he had to make a decision, one he thought was already made for him.

The newly awarded hometown hero stood quiet yet amazed in the town cemetery. He stood alert in his full military uniform and newly shining medals and was all but speechless. George was wearing his full military uniform for this special event. The cemetery George was standing in, however, was not special. It looked exactly how he remembered it, long, flat, and cold. The gray and black headstones lined the rows for what seemed like miles. Only the variation in stone sizes separated one plot from the next. The green and brown grass lined most of the graves, except for the most recent ones. The grass was almost perfect, and it made George wonder, *funny how the grass grows so alive in a place that's full of death!* Most of the stones were solo and quiet, although some had flowers and rocks and other items topping their bow. The perfect rows of death seemed to line up in harmony like a good tune that you could not get out of your head. The wind would whistle through the stones, causing flowers to blow, but it presented a peaceful tune to George as he stood overlooking the eternal resting places of so many people. The perfect grass also ran up to the edge of his toes, and that's where the perfection stopped. Dirt still lay in bump form at the bottom of his feet. Only a few blades had begun to grow in this spot, indicating death had yet to take this soul.

Just moments earlier, George was honored with a parade and a ceremony from his hometown of White City. The town was small, but the crowd that showed up to honor Stone was huge. He recognized some of the town folk, but many others he did not. The crowd wanted to hear his stories of survival behind enemy lines and how he was able to get back. However, that was not the story George wanted to tell. George wanted to tell a story of love's survival, but that story did not have an ending. Stone was now a war hero, but the story that made him so special had nothing to do with the war. It had everything to do with the decision he would soon have to make: forget about Stone Chapel or try to go back one last time.

Several months earlier, George asked for a return trip to Calais, France, where he had been for nearly two years. But much to his disappointment, the request was turned down. The United States closed down all borders to that area so France could reclaim and rebuild their land. There was now an eight-year blackout for travel to that part of the country, and George did not know what to do. He was not even sure if the person he was so desperate to see was still there, still alive, or even wanted to see him. George had been liberated by his own country and then taken away on a plane back to London before he'd ever regained consciousness. Probably a good thing, as George would have fought to the death to reclaim what was his.

But what happened to the woman that he had fallen in love with? *Did she return to the cabin?* He often wondered. There were just too many questions without answers for Stone as he looked down at the dirt and rock at his feet. It was a gravestone ... with *his* name on it. George Stone was reported killed in a plane crash a couple of years ago, and his family held a funeral service for him. Now he was back from the dead and had a new chance to start his life all over again. The gravestone would soon be dug up and removed, as there was obviously no body buried underneath it. *I'll be in there someday just not right now!* He thought as he looked down. There was also a second newly presented gravestone. It was three down from Stone's, and it read *Dale Messing, war hero, town friend to all.*

It was hard for George to walk down to Dale's plot. Dale was his best friend and the man he went off to war with. George used to get mad at his friend because Dale had a tendency to talk too much. What George wouldn't give to hear his voice right now? But George knew Dale would not be coming back. He knew Dale was dead ... he had witnessed it.

Standing alone, George knew he owed it to his friend to walk down and look at his headstone. George turned and took a few steps toward the second rock. He walked up to the stone and knelt over it. He reached into his pocket and pulled out a small pocketknife and slid it open. The rusted knife fought to expose itself, but George was able to push the metal to a full open and ready position. This was the position and the knife that once saved Stone's life, and he was very grateful for it. He took the knife and placed it open onto the top of the rock near Dale's name. He nodded but could not find any words to say as he crouched down and stared at the headstone. He took his left hand, rubbed his eyes, and slid his right hand along the letters of

Dale's name. He knew Dale was not in this grave, but this stone would not be removed; Dale was gone.

George reached and grabbed part of his military shirt and used it to wipe his eyes as a couple of tears slid down his cheek. He would soon be talking to his lifelong friends who were waiting for him outside the fence, and the last thing he wanted was for them to see him cry. George slowly stood back up and turned to his family, who was standing some three hundred yards away. They were all silent and all looking at him as he turned and began walking toward them. He passed back by his headstone one last time then stopped and turned to it. He stared for a few seconds, and that was the point he decided to try and give Stone Chapel one last try. It would be eight years before he could make any contact. There was no address at the cabin, so a letter to France would be fruitless. If this were to work and if this were truly meant to be, he would need to be there in person.

George got a small smile on his face and began mentally planning the trip that he would take some eight years from this moment. He left the cemetery and walked over to an older woman who was standing outside the gate. Her dress was black, her skin was white, her face pale as the snow. Her hair was white on the sides but covered by a dark brown wig she had pinned to her black veil. George noticed she had been crying, so he walked up to her and embraced her.

"Dale was a great friend. I will miss him the rest of my life," he told the woman while pulling her close to his chest and giving her a kiss on the head. It was Dale's grandmother, with whom George had always held a special bond. Despite the sad moments in the cemetery, George left feeling full of life and optimistic about his return to Stone Chapel.

The Beginning, Her Father
Dover, England
1937

The wind was more popular than the town residents during this late afternoon hour. It might as well have been midnight for the loss of people and business that had left the town this day. The village was now an arena lined by wood and steel on each side and running the length of the town. The spectators were not in open seating and were not waiting to cheer. Instead, they were hidden behind the windows and mortar that made up the country shacks. These city followers were loyal to the leader, but their loyalties only stretched as far as their front door on this day ... and that was just to get a better view. The men in the streets were on their own. People rarely entered the walk or even left their homes or businesses when men like this took to the streets. Despite their absence on this bleak day, the eyes of this small town weighed heavily on the shoulders of Richard Wild.

As he stood in the middle of the street, rifle softly at his right side, the country wind blew through his hair. His dark black hat was blowing lightly every few seconds, but his eyes were focused and his hands were steady. His brown leather jacket was lined with scrapes and scars that were common for this type of work. A rip here, a bullet hole there. This particular trench coat stretched all the way to the bottom of his boots. It was also a treasured piece of cloth because it belonged to his father, who had worn it to fight in many victorious battles. His boots peeked from the bottom of his untied coat and his face lay tan, silent, and rough. He had not shaved in several days but appeared young enough that most people would not notice. And while the forty-two years on his body were not deep, the notches on his rifle were.

He was a man who had unwillingly followed in his father's footsteps but kept the peace and the values that his father held dear. Richard was not a man of violence until he needed to be. He was not a man of revenge until it was called for. He was not a man of God until God called to him. If he were lucky, that would not happen for at least a few more minutes. His brown hair caught the edge of the sun and appeared blonde to the tips. His deep blue eyes were hidden by the brow of his hat as the shadow cast across them. He was a man the town loved, feared, and respected more than any other resident. If he died this day, their world would change forever. This was not the old west in America; just the opposite—it was England. But the non-bending tales and legends from the American old west had encouraged new stories, and these tales had made their way to England. The town of Dover was about to discover what had happened in Dodge City, America, some five decades earlier. Change was on the horizon, and Wild was the man trying to make it happen. Yet some men, even ones who shared his blood, refused to let this happen. For some reason they had a debt to collect, and Richard Wild was their cashier.

Other than the quiet whisper of the wind, the only sounds heard were the popping and crackling of his fingers as he squeezed them in and out while holding the rifle. Soon this street would be quiet. The sound of death was a sound he was hoping to hear. To Richard that would mean this was finally over. This middle-aged man had spent the last few weeks in torment. He had waited for this moment, and now the opportunity was upon him. The men standing three doorsteps down were strangers to Richard, but at least one of them shared the same blood. And that blood would spill one way or another on this day. As the brave men stood staring at each other, waiting for someone to make a move, a distant screen door was starting to slap in the wind. A horse, scared by the wind, started to shake and jump. But Richard did not see or hear anything on this brisk evening. His attention was totally focused on the men standing in front of him. A town full of anticipation and glaring eyes was waiting for someone to surrender, but Richard would not waver in his resolve. All he thought about was the three men he was about to kill … or be killed by.

Then he recalled how he got to this point.

DOVER, ENGLAND
THREE MONTHS EARLIER

The flint hills that lined the homestead were as green as the stems on the roses that lined the brick house. The land was large, but from a distance, it appeared miniature. It was the world to the Wild family and all they really cared about. Richard Wild was working to fix a portion of the fence that had recently fallen down in one of the frequent storms. The fence did not really need fixing; it was in bad shape. But that's how Richard Wild was; when there was a problem, he liked to get it fixed and out of the way right away. He was not a perfectionist per se, but he was a stickler for procrastination. He did not like it, he did not like people who did it, and he was so bothered by it that some nights he couldn't sleep if he knew there was a job that needed to be completed. To say Richard Wild was an impatient man was like saying the world was round. This might have been his biggest downfall.

Wild looked up from the job he had dedicated most of his morning to and veered down the way. It was easy to tell someone was approaching the ranch. In the distance, behind the long-tipped green trees surrounding the winding road, the dust began to stir. Richard tipped his black-billed cowboy hat and looked up from his current job. His dirty blue eyes strained to focus through the sweat that had collected on his face. He tried to focus and see through the dust and sun to discover who was headed his way, but it was a fruitless venture. He reached down and placed the end of the fence on the ground. Normally this proud, rugged man would not be wearing his dirty work clothes but rather a dusty pair of boots and old jeans. However, today Richard had already conducted business. He had already been out most of the morning and had just returned, hoping to finish the front fence. On most days the fence was all that protected his young family from the outside, and in his line of business, they needed protection.

Richard was a dangerous man. It was not a title he really ever wanted but was cast into the role fulltime after his father's murder. Colonel Thurman Wild was probably the biggest name in these parts of twentieth-century England. He was the law, or at least the version of the law around here. The colonel was a World War I hero who settled his family in this small town. It was not his home, but his family never claimed much of anywhere as home. The colonel had actually been born and raised in a cabin in the mountains on the other side of the channel in France. When the colonel died of an unexpected illness, a bullet to the back of the head, his name and title, as well as his debts, passed on to his son Richard. The younger Wild had hopes of being a rancher, and that is how he spent his spare time. His father was the law in this town, and when he died, it was a natural transition for town folks to look to Richard Wild for protection. Wild never took the badge, but he did take on the responsibility and promised to avenge his father's death.

Richard could tell by the soft rattle of the metal chains hitting the wheels and the rattling of the gas engine that a motorized wagon was headed to the ranch. While Richard still favored riding a horse, he realized that everyone was driving automobiles these days. Richard had gotten his first taste of motorized wagons a few years earlier when his father brought one home.

The dust grew closer and thicker with each passing second. The Wild family was not expecting any guests, so Richard quickly turned and walked back to the house to pick up his rifle that was sitting on the porch. As he approached the house, the dog, maybe more dangerous than the weapon, lifted his head. The favored sidekick looked for some sweet satisfaction from his friend in the form of a pat on the head. When one was not offered, the dog became alerted to possible danger and began to focus on the action in front of him.

"We got company?" a woman's voice asked, coming from an upstairs window.

"Looks that way," Richard resolved. "Send Eve down here with the Winchester."

Richard picked up his rifle and slid it under his right arm … his shooting arm. He reached down and wiped some dirt off his hand onto his shirt.

Gliding up behind the man most called "Wild," a young girl quickly came out the front door carrying a rifle. She was dressed in a familiar pair of jean overalls and a red shirt that still had wrinkle marks lining the sleeves. She was no taller than the man's neck but appeared as big as life as she stood holding the large weapon that was nearly as tall as her. Her hair tossed a bit in the wind as she closed one eye, lined up her target, and then relaxed the rifle back down. She wore the boots of a young man, but her body showed signs that she was no boy. This young woman was now eighteen years old, and while it was a bit odd for her to not be in a relationship, she never thought twice about it—at least when her father was around.

"Where do you want me?" asked his daughter, who was named Eve.

"Just stay on the porch. I'll do the talking," Richard ordered. Eve slowly stepped to the right and firmly put the weapon under her arm as the family pet raised to all fours.

Step-by-step, Wild walked backwards toward the front fence as if to time the arrival of the approaching auto. With the rifle ready under his arm and the sweat lining the rim of his well-worn black hat, Richard was cautious as to the news he was about to hear. *Would he soon be returning to work, or was this less important?* In his business it really didn't matter. For him most of the stories were the same, and he had heard them all.

From the trees that lined the front of the home an automobile appeared. With the rattling of the engine and the dirt flowing from the tires, it was clear this trip was made especially for Richard.

There was a lone driver guiding the car onto the front lawn of the Wild home. Richard cracked a half smile as he recognized the driver. It was as the local postman. It was a man he'd see once every couple of weeks but never at his home.

The man pulled hard on the wooden steering wheel, and the auto came to a stop right in front of the fencepost that Richard had been repairing just moments earlier. The motorized wagon was old, even for this time, black, and covered in dust and to Richard a very loud distraction. The engine's only purpose this day seemed to be disturbing the peace, but its visit was for a very special reason. The rattling of the engine quickly quieted as the driver killed the engine.

Wild took the weapon from under his arm and sat it against the fence post. The other rifle was still lapped over his neck, as he was always in a ready state to handle any trouble that arose.

"Hello, Peter," Richard offered.

"Wild," the man replied as he ruffled though a bag that was sitting in the seat next to him.

"Kind of a long trip out here on such a nice day. You must have some special mail for me," Richard said with a smile.

"Not too sure. It's a sealed telegraph I received for you. Came straight from up north. It looks important." He continued to fumble through a leather pouch that was next to him and eventually pulled out a strange and mysterious envelope. He carefully handed it to Richard as if it were a fragile porcelain doll. The telegram appeared as normal as any other, but this one seemed to have special interest. This one carried information that might soon change the world the Wild had come to know.

"When are you going to fix this fence?" asked the postman as he walked to his car.

"Soon!" replied Richard. "From up north, huh? I don't know anyone up there!" Richard looked over the gift and then slid it into a large, sagging pocket that was on his red-plaid shirt just above his chest.

"Thanks for coming all this way. Can I get you a drink?"

"No thanks, love to make the trips like this. Especially when it's not too hot. Anyway, best I be getting on. I've got more stops to make. This letter seemed important enough that I get it to you right away. Hope it's good news."

The postman reached down and turned a key, re-starting the rattling engine. He then turned the hard wooden steering wheel, and the engine that had been quiet for a brief moment started rattling again. The auto began to drive back down the road from which it came. The dust was kicking up from this end this time. Richard brushed his hand in front of his face to rid the dirt and then reached into his pocket and pulled out the envelope. He stuck one end in his teeth, ripped a corner, and then pulled the cracking paper from inside. Wild had no idea what the letter could be about.

Richard pulled the paper from the torn envelope. It was a telegram. His eyes began to squint as he read the vital message. His eyebrows began to bend as his face got a bewildered look.

His wife yelled to him, "What's it say, Richard? Who's it from?"

While holding the envelope, Richard slowly pulled his arm down from his face. He turned back to the women he loved. "I'm heading up north."

Part 2

His Return
Calais, France
1953

Cla-clunk, cla-clunk, cla-clunk. That was the sound coming from the wheels of the rickety old railroad train as George Stone sat quietly glaring out of the open-air window. The sun dominated his right side and cast a glow through the open passenger cabin onto his right leg.

The sun made the seat incredibly hot, and a number of other passengers on the train were beginning to sweat. George noticed a woman wearing a large animal-skinned hat. *She must be burning up*, he thought. There were several other passengers on the train, but George was not bothered with any of their stories. He had his own. He had his own personal reason for being on the train, and it was one he was not about to share with anyone. His past had more recently dominated his current thoughts. He felt that now was the time to relieve the inner stress that had built up over the past eight years.

George turned once again to the window and listened patiently to the soft, constantly rotating sounds of the train. Cla-clunk, cla-clunk, cla-clunk. With each passing tree George could almost time the exact moment the next wheel would cry its familiar tune. Each passing tree was identical to the one before, green and plump with leaves. As George looked down the track, he could see the pattern in the trees where the train had worn on them over time. The trees were close enough to touch. All he would have to do was hold his hand out and feel the cool leaves as they passed across his fingers. But therein lay the danger. A branch could pop out from behind a hidden bush and take off his arm. George had become very conservative over the last several years, and that was why he was so surprised that he was able to come back to this country that he had been forced so quickly to abandon years earlier.

George knew this would be his one opportunity, his one chance to put back in his hand what he had lost—the touch of the woman that he loved.

The trip seemed endless to George. For the past few days, he had been on a bus, a train, and several airplanes before reaching his final destination. *It didn't seem this hard to get here last time,* he joked to himself. But George had already spent a lifetime looking for his true love and when he found her … she was abruptly taken away. That was why George was on this train, that was why George had traveled so far, and that was why George was willing to return to the country that had held him captive eight years earlier. It was for the love of a woman.

Stone, dressed in what appeared to be a businessman's suit and tie, began to hurt from the bottom side. He was feeling several pains coming from his ass. Unlike the seat on the airplane, this seat had no padding. It was a hard wooden bench meant for short travel, not a long trip. George had already spent more time on the train than anyone else on it. He had witnessed people load and unload at least four times since he got onto the train. He did have the best seat, though. Right next to the big window with a nice, cool breeze blowing into the train cabin and right onto his face. The wind blowing on him was a blessing because it helped hide some of the odor he was beginning to release.

The scenery was beautiful. It was a view that he did not remember seeing the last time he was in this country. Although the beauty would have been hard to notice as the last time he was in France; he was at war, and this place was in ruins. George was an American soldier behind enemy lines, and this land was still absolutely terrifying to him. But now the land was as peaceful as the smooth air that was hitting his face. Only the beauty of her face in his thoughts topped the beautiful view, one he hoped he would soon be seeing. The sky was her hair … long and flowing until the end of time. The trees were as green and comforting as her eyes. The flowers along the tracks were as red as her lips and just as soft to the touch. It was obvious his Eve still lived in these hills, even if she was not physically right in front of him.

Cla-clunk, cla-clunk … whoooooooo, the train whistle blew. George was getting closer to finding his answer, and the anticipation was killing him. *Would she still be there? Would she still remember him? Would she remember their silent promise and still wear the small ring he had once made for her?* His ring was lost to the war, but he was hoping she would not be.

As the train continued on its long journey, George felt a sense of relief. He was glad that his government, the United States, had once again allowed foreign travel to Europe. It took George eight years to finally be given the okay and get his passport approved for travel back to this place that he had once longed to leave.

As a soldier you are taught one thing, George convinced himself. *Not get too attached to anything or anyone during times of war, because sometimes the life after can be worse than death.*

Cla-clunk, cla-clunk, cla-clunk. The continued rotating sound was beginning to put George to sleep. The soft sounds of the train and the moving motion reminded George of the last time he was on a train, or at least was about to get on one. He crossed his arms and laid his head back as his eyelids became too heavy to stay open.

KANSAS, AMERICA
1942

George Stone was always nervous just before a big trip, and this one was the biggest of his life. Stone was so nervous that he'd spent the previous ten minutes at his home hovering over the marble mule in the bathroom releasing his breakfast. But he somehow managed to hide his feeling as he headed out for the depot.

Stone made his way down the short path from his home. He walked by the cemetery without looking that way and then slowed and approached the train depot that was in the center of his hometown in White City, Kansas. George had spent many younger years playing around the cemetery and never seemed to have an issue with it until today. He knew if he looked over to it he might discover more of the ham and eggs that had stayed behind from the last visit.

This was truly a small town, but it was cluttered with people and uniforms and families on this special day. The train was sitting quietly in the port as the steam slowly rose up around its massive iron wheels. George had seen trains before but never one that looked or felt so important ... and cold. The United States Army logo was on the side of the huge rust-colored metal beast, followed by a monster-sized white star. As George walked up to the depot, he felt a little intimidated, yet proud all at the same time. This was the day that all of the army recruits were set to load up on the train and head out for war. The train had begun its journey in California and would end near New York. All along the way more soldiers, more young brave souls would step aboard, ready to do whatever it took to fight for their country's freedom.

George was one of these soldiers. He had never thought of joining the army. Moreover, his father was a farmer and that was all he knew. George figured farming was his future. But after his close friend Dale signed up, George thought he too owed it to his country.

The young soldier stopped near the dock and turned his head the length of the train. He could not see the end from either side. It was long and dark, reminding him of a coffin.

I hope I can get a good seat! The young boy said to himself quietly.

George noticed that nearly every other soldier was dressed just like him. He was wearing standard army gray and green with a helmet and a large duffel bag. He was also wearing bright shiny new black boots, and his smile proved just how proud he really was.

George had packed a few essentials, mostly long wool underwear. He knew he was headed for Germany or somewhere in Europe. Either way, it was very cold there in the winter. George had also packed lots of paper and envelopes so he could write his parents while he was away. He even packed away a large bag of dried beef jerky that his mother had just made for him. He knew it would be a long trip, and he did not know what to expect.

Just two months earlier, George received his U.S. Army uniform upon completion of boot camp. He was given a pass to return to Kansas and get his business in order before he was called to duty. While at training camp, George and his friend Dale signed on to join Stars and Stripes, the United States Army official news agency. The two had learned a little about journalism while working on Dale's uncle's newspaper as students in school. George's uncle ran the local paper, and Dale's father worked for him. Dale had learned to write from his dad and was going to write for the Stars and Stripes paper. George was learning a new skill called filming. George's army career choice was news cameraman. The army had given him at least a hundred rolls of film he tucked securely in his duffel bag. He would get his camera once he got his assignment.

What George really liked about Stars and Stripes was that he would get the opportunity to work with several different units all over Europe. George and Dale would get to be together and join different troops at different locations. They would get their story, shoot some film, spend time with that unit, and then pick up with another. It was kind of like a vacation. They would get to see all the good stuff and film it for the people back home in the States. George really liked that idea.

While George stood watching many of the soldiers load onto the train, he could also see some of the other men already on board through the window. He noticed that a couple of them were crying as they glared out the window.

That will be me soon, he thought. That's when he felt something jag him in the back.

"Stick 'em up soldier!" said a familiar voice. George turned and laughed, knowing it was his friend Dale. He knew his voice well because he'd heard it often. Dale liked to talk. I mean he really liked to talk. There were very few issues that Dale Messing did not have an opinion on, and he was not shy about discussing them with others. Still, Dale was a trusted friend and one every young man in an American uniform was looking for on this day. They sought a friend to watch their backs when they could not. None of these kids from who collected at the depot this day had ever been to war. The only killing most had done in the past was of a coyote trying to attack their chickens. Now they were being asked to protect something much bigger than their poultry ... their country.

"It's about time you got here. The train's set to leave in five minutes," George stated.

"I've been here all along," Dale explained. "My folks are right down there. They're talking to yours," he added while his arm was extended, pointing to their families. Dale was a good bit shorter than George and a few months older. His hair was darker but other than size, he looked just like his buddy standing next to him in the brand-new uniform. The two had been best friends their entire life and had considered this the next logical step for them to take.

George appeared a little distressed.

"I said good-bye to them back at the house; what are they doing here?" he asked. "Now I'm going to cry if I have to say good-bye again!"

"I'd like to see that!" added Dale. "You look like a girl when you cry ... all boo-hoo!!" Dale made sad face expressions as he joked with his best friend.

"Come on! Cut it out! You are just as sad as I am about leaving here," George retorted.

"No way. I can't wait to get on that train. You and I are going to see the world, man. I've only been to four other counties in this state ... well, and Missouri, but I didn't want to go there. This is our ticket out of here!" Dale assured his friend as he patted George on the shoulder.

The two young soldiers turned and walked down to their families that had gathered to say good-bye. There were six family members standing and smiling as they walked up. George immediately looked to his mother. She was packed in warm clothing with at least two jackets. Her eyes were red from crying, and her hat was blowing in the wind. George also noticed his father. While he had not shed a tear, George could tell his father was deeply saddened to see his young son leave. George's younger sister Elizabeth was also with the family. She was the one he would probably miss the most. His job was to take care of her and watch over her. She was just thirteen years old, and there were a lot of ways to get hurt in the country. George was now twenty and was the only remaining brother to Elizabeth. Their other sibling, Jonathan, would have been eighteen this winter but had died of pneumonia two winters earlier. His death nearly tore the family apart. That was the day George truly grew up; the day his brother died.

Along with the Stones stood Dale's family, the Messings. Their families were pretty close. Both fathers had been good friends growing up, as were their fathers before them. The families were cut from the same mold. George and Dale were third-generation best friends. Neither was too concerned about the war. They were both admittedly naïve, but both of their fathers fought in a war and came back unharmed. Plus their job would be a fun one. They would never be on the frontline. Instead, they would be covering the story from a distance, a lucky break for the two best friends.

"I thought we just did this?" George said to his parents, who were standing in front of him. His dad was dressed in his rarely seen dark black suit and a rounded fitted flat hat. His mother was also dressed in black. She wore a black dress underneath two outer coats to protect her from the wind chill. His younger sister stood next to her mother, also wrapped in a heavy winter coat. Her white dress with a flower design peaked out from under the coat down past her knees. George realized his sister was the only one not wearing black. This gave him a warm feeling because he did not think this was an occasion for black to be worn. Black was attire for a funeral.

"We did, but we just couldn't let you go without giving you a gift," answered his father.

"What gift?" he asked. His mother reached out her arm to him.

"This one," she said.

George looked down to see a small wristwatch with a black material band and was ticking as if it were brand new. The hands of the clock were shaped like little swords, and there was a picture of Saint Peter behind the hands, outlined in a white background. George took the watch from his mother and slowly raised it to his eyes to see it better.

"You didn't have to do that," he said in a proud voice.

"Behold Saint Peter and go your way in safety, my son," his mother cried softly.

The young Stone got a big grin on his face that no other human had and then wrapped the new watch around his wrist. George had a grin that his family and friends had fallen in love with. It was a grin that was so unique that anyone who knew him could quickly pick it out, and they knew exactly what it meant: he was truly happy. This made his parents feel a little more secure about their son heading off to war. They both began to smile proudly, as they knew their son took pride in his gift.

"Where's my watch?" Dale comically asked his father. They all laughed as a huge whistle blew.

Whhoooooooooo. The bells began to sound … ding, ding, ding.

"Oh, we've got to go!" said Dale as the large iron wheels slowly began to turn and let out a large screech.

The two young soldiers hugged each of their family members one last time, knowing it might be their last but having the heart not to mention it. Then the brave young men took off for the train. They went up the loading ramp and jumped onto the side stairs of one train car. They both waved back to their families as the train pulled out of the depot and continued its trip onward toward the east coast.

As they looked and waved, Dale turned to George.

"Do you think we'll ever see this place again?" he asked in a calm voice.

"I sure hope so," answered George with a large smile from cheek to cheek.

The long dark train pulled out of White City for the final time. Only the large stars painted on the side could be seen clearly as the engine picked up speed then vanished off into the distance. George's mother would stand in that same spot the rest of the day.

THE JOURNEY
EUROPE
1943

The constant rotating roar of the super beast army cargo plane, the c-137 engine, was all that George Stone could hear as he sat in the belly of the large metal flying animal. There were no windows anywhere close to him. Not that a window would have mattered much, as it was pitch dark outside anyway. George was sitting on a bench made out of canvas that folded down from the inner wall of the plane. It was long, stretching nearly the entire length of the plane. Stone was sitting really close to the door. In fact, not a single soldier separated him from it. To his right, sitting nearly elbow to elbow, were over two hundred more army men dressed just like him, helmet and parachute in tow. Across from him were two hundred more soldiers lining that inner wall.

George turned his head and looked around the inside of the dark plane. The red lights illuminating the floor cast the only light onto the four hundred or so soldiers who were eagerly sitting in the plane. George could smell the fear that encompassed the plane. It was a smell his nose had picked up before. More than anything it was body sweat from wearing the same clothes for such a long period of time, but George refused to think of the smell as odor. To him it was fear because he was thinking the same thing everyone else was, and it was making him nervous. George did not feel the same urgency as the others because he was aware of his mission. While shooting was involved, it was with a film camera and not on the frontline with a rifle. He was, however, going to have to jump out of this plane, and that was something he had never done before. *Will they be shooting at us in the air?* George thought. He was not sure; he had never been in this spot before.

George continued to turn his head and take a quick glance at each soldier sitting across from him, at least until it was too dark to make out a face. He could see the look of anxiety on every face as his eyes panned the group—at least on the ones who were awake. Others were sleeping, and this was also a clue for George to figure out. *How could they be sleeping at a time like this?* He thought. He did not know it at the time but would later understand: the sleepers were the veterans. They were the smart ones because they had been through this before. The sleepers knew to rest as much as possible because soon they would not enjoy the comfort of sleep. Little did they know that the images they would see in battle would rob them of sleep for many, many years to come. Sleep was a silent blessing on this flight. The rotating engines made for a nice calming mood in what otherwise would have been a nerve-wracking four hours on this canvas bench. Yes, the precious sleeping hours were the final hours of bliss and getaway from a mission that was about to begin.

Still, there was a sense of harmony for the soldiers who were sitting side by side on the long metal and canvas bench that lined both sides of the inner plane. All the soldiers were fully loaded up, complete with helmets, supply bags, and parachutes attached to their backs. They were dressed in their standard issue green and black and were almost willing to accept whatever fate lay ahead of them. This was a mission that some would not come back from, and George could read it in the face of every person when they had loaded up on that plane some three and a half hours earlier.

Across from George sat a smiling Dale Messing, his best friend. Dale was excited because this was their first real assignment together. In just over two months the two had shot and reported a number of stories around the foreign base and workout areas, but they had never been assigned a real mission, a mission that meant something. It was a chance for George and his good friend to tell the story of the boys on the frontline—the boys that would be parachuting in behind enemy lines and seeing the fruits of live action firsthand. This was the story that Dale had been waiting for but not George. He was more than a little concerned about the jump they were about to make. They had made jumps before in training, but this would be their first real jump into enemy lines. It would be the first real jump where someone might be shooting at them. And to add to George's displeasure, he'd chosen the low number as they were about to board the plane. That meant he was first in line to jump out of the plane, and Dale would be close behind ... about four hundred feet behind, as he was the last in the line. As George looked at Dale, he understood why his closest friend in the world was smiling ... because *he* was the first one out of the plane!

The two young journalists had been with this unit for about a week and were fitting in pretty well. The assignment was simple. The group was to drop in behind enemy lines and hold a bridge until a back support of tanks could arrive. It was supposed to be a three-day mission. But there were more planes than just this one. In fact, as George boarded the plane, he'd counted at least eleven other planes flying the same mission. Sure, he was upset about being the first to jump out of the plane, but at least he would have a pretty good view going down ... no one in front of him to block the scenery.

As George continued to glance around the plane, he noticed that Dale was pointing to something off to his left just over George's shoulder. He looked around but did not see anything. He looked back to Dale as his friend started to point again. The plane was too loud for conversation, even at the short ten feet they sat apart. George looked back and shook his shoulders as if to tell Dale he didn't know what he was pointing at. Dale looked back and shook his head back and forth. He used his hands to make a small circle and held it up to his eyes. He looked through his handmade window and then pointed back over George's shoulder. George turned to the door that was next to him and noticed a small window near the top. He turned back to Dale and shook his head, finally understanding him. Then he stood up, slightly bending his body backward to get a glimpse out of the small glass-filled hole. He was the only one who was able to see out of the window because he was so close to it. For anyone else to see through it, he would have to get up and step out of line. This was not possible because every soldier was wearing a parachute that was hooked to a long wire that ran the length of the plane. The wire would pull the chute for the soldiers the minute they jumped out of the plane. This was needed because it was a low-level jump, less than five hundred feet, so there would not be time for a free fall and pull. If your chute did not open right after you jumped out of the plane, you would be dead before a bullet ever hit your body.

So as it turned out George was actually the luckiest man on the plane. He might actually be able to have a view other than a soldier sitting and staring back at him from across the aisle.

George leaned up toward the window and was able to get his entire face in it. Still, it was very dark, and there was not a lot to see. The ground was black, so he was not sure where it began and the sky ended, although there were a couple of low-level clouds passing by. He strained his eyes a bit and could see blinking lights from at least three other planes off to the side, flying at different heights but at the same speed.

George looked down at his watch and could see from the soft red light that it was 10:38 p.m. He looked back at Dale, who was still smiling back at him from across the plane.

"What time are we supposed to jump?" George asked while twisting his fingers in agony. But due to the extreme noise in the plane and the roar of the engine, Dale could not hear George. He simply shrugged back as if to not be able to hear him and pointed to his ears. George realized the problem and then laughed a little and looked back out the window. Stone was having a hard time staying glued to the window because the weight on his feet kept shifting back and forth. The plane was beginning to shake, rocking slowly back and forth. However, this did not concern the two friends because it had been doing the same thing since they had taken off some three hours earlier.

George looked up as he heard some rattling that sounded like it was coming from the plane. He could not quite figure out what it was, but he knew something was wrong. *There it is again!* George heard the rattling for a second time. He looked around to see if anyone else heard the noise, but no one seemed to be affected. He looked back to Dale and pointed to his ears and then shook his head as if to ask if he could hear it. Dale shrugged his shoulders and reached into his pocket. He pulled out a small pocketknife and opened it up. He reached back into his coat pocket and pulled out a piece of dried meat and cut the meat into small pieces and placed them in his mouth. Meanwhile, George put both his hands on the plane and then moved his ear close to it. The helmet he was wearing prevented him from putting his ear on the door by the small window. George tried to isolate the smooth engine noise from what he thought was rattling. He stared down the body of the plane as his helmet continued to bump on the door as he shook and then heard it again.

Ratt ... ratt ... ratt ... ting ... ting ... ting ... ting ... it sounded like thousands of little metals dings hitting the plane. Then he looked up and noticed one of the soldiers sitting next to Dale had fallen asleep. The soldier leaned down quickly, and as George took a closer look at him, he noticed that blood was coming from the soldier's mouth. The soldier had been shot, and the only thing holding him up was the tie from his parachute to the order line. At that moment George realized the rattling sound was bullets hitting the plane.

George began to get frantic as he tried to explain to Dale they were under attack. Dale turned to his friend and slowly pulled his hand and the knife down from his mouth. He looked at George as he quickly pointed to the solider that had been shot. George tried to get Dale to see the blood coming from his mouth, but that was when the explosions started outside the plane.

Ka-boom ... boom ... boom.

Ground rockets were exploding around the plane. The pilot of the plane turned the aircraft back and forth to dodge the explosions. The soldiers who lined the plane were trying to hold on as the plane swayed from side to side. Dale's smile quickly turned to concern as he fought to hang onto the line that was attached to his chute. George noticed that one of his sergeants at the other end of the plane had unhooked himself and started stumbling along the line of the troops, but George could not tell what he was saying.

Ka-boom ... boom ... boom ... the explosions were getting louder and more frequent. George looked out of the small window on the door but did not see the other aircraft that had been flying alongside. His plane seemed to be alone and had possibly flown off course. According to George's calculations, they were headed the wrong direction.

As the explosions lit up the sky, George could see what appeared to be a couple of large mountains and a large body of water off in the distance. He could also feel his stomach lowering into his waist, telling him the plane was climbing into the pitch-black sky.

As he turned his head back and looked at Dale, the window he had just been looking through shattered and blew out after being struck by a stray bullet. The shattered window caused a vacuum leak, and all the air was sucking toward the door. George closed his eyes in fear and grabbed a hold of the line that was attached to his parachute. Dale was holding on as well, but some of the other soldiers fell on the floor and were struggling to get back on the bench as the plane continued to rock back and forth and then climb and descend. Then suddenly a large explosion rocked the plane and turned it sideways.

Ka-boom!

The explosion was so great that it blew out the door that George was sitting next to. The door was sucked out of the plane and into the darkness. George fell to his feet and was pulled to the door and out into the darkness right behind the large metal door. As he slid out, his eye caught Dale's, and both were stuck in a split second of hell, one thinking he was about the die and the other thinking he was about to lose his best friend. George's parachute was still attached to the line, and he was dangling just outside the plane as the explosions became more intense. Most of the soldiers began to scream and yell as they held on for dear life to avoid being sucked out of the plane as well. The sergeant who had just moments earlier been walking in the plane was quickly sliding toward the door. Two other strapped-in soldiers grabbed his legs and got a hold of him to keep him from flying out of the exposed area.

Meanwhile, George was flopping back and forth outside the plane. His body became an uncontrollable flag flopping in the wind. Dale knew his best friend would not be able to survive much longer being dragged outside the plane. The brave soldier, still attached to the wire and somehow still holding the small pocketknife, fought his way across the aisle to the line that was holding George. Dale could see his friend's legs flopping outside the door and began to cry as he leaned over to cut the line. He realized that George had a better chance of surviving on his own. Dale knew George was just seconds away from death if he did not cut the line soon.

Outside the plane George was starting to lose consciousness as his body was being continually slammed against the plane. His lungs were becoming so overcome by the hard wind that he found it difficult to breathe. If not for the helmet strapped tightly to his head, he would surely be dead by now.

Inside the plane Dale was lying on the floor and pulling himself as far as he could. Still attached to the wire, he frantically cut the line that was still attached to the jump cord of the plane and his best friend, George. He hoped his friend was still alive and not too badly mangled from the beating he had taken from the plane. With a final strong cut, the line snapped. The cord quickly fled the plane, and George was shot away from his capture. His parachute automatically opened, but he was too high and could not get a grasp on the direction he was headed. In the pure darkness, he looked back to the plane that was now in solo flight and battled the explosions that seemed to land closer and closer to it. The plane continued to fight the air explosions as it flew farther away from the parachuted solider who was slowly gliding down and heading for a mountain in the distance.

Even though his eyelids were frozen and beginning to turn white, he kept watching the plane until … one of the rockets connected with it.

Kaboom … The plane was hit.

George hung alone in the darkness as the home he had known for the past few hours had just been struck and was falling apart in the air. It was a light show like no other. The cold, dark night sky lit up like a full red moon as the aircraft disintegrated into dozens of pieces flying in every direction. If George had more time to think about it, he would have realized that his best friend from the time he had been born had just died. Not only had his best friend just perished, but he had also saved George's life. It was a debt that George could never repay.

Yet George was still in shock from the last few seconds that had changed his life. He was about to parachute deep behind enemy lines with nothing more than a supply bag and a rifle with limited ammunition. He also had a handgun with less than thirty rounds and a film camera all set to start shooting the action of war. George looked straight down; he was about to drop into heavy brush covered in snow. *What a beautiful view, what a horrible day,* he thought. The treetops were completely covered in white, and while it was pitch dark on this mountainside, he could see the snow as clear as day. He quickly looked up one last time at the remains of the plane falling to the ground some five miles away. That's when it hit him that Dale was still on that plane and that *George* was the only one who was able to get out of the certain death.

No one would come for me; everyone would think that I died on that plane, he thought. His train of thought also brought many other questions: *did the German soldiers see me parachute out? Would they come looking for me? Is it true I am on my own?* He hurt all over, but the certain loss of his friend hurt more. However, he had to push aside those feelings because now it was all about survival. George was now on his own. The long parachute and the newly awarded soldier disappeared into a massive forest area on the side of the mountain. The open chute suddenly collapsed, and he fell though the tree, bringing the young American soldier to his new home.

Six Hours Later

The cold winter wind blew hard and close to the ground, kicking up snow and drifting it as a small patch of darkness worked its way out from under the white blanket. The patch slowly rose from the ground and began to uncover itself slightly, first unveiling a set of deep blue eyes casting out from a dirty white face dripping in sweat. They were as solid and concentrated as the snow that lay on top of them and yet so focused they did not blink. Slowly a complete face rose out of the snow, and the morning light calmly welcomed it. Small stacks of clumped snow began to dissipate as the body that had been hidden so cleverly in snow slowly came into view. This may have been a snow angel, but it was not a face familiar to these parts. If the snow had not covered this foreign body, many unknown dangers may have come to it. The body, which had been lying face down in the snow, now rose to a knee-hold position. His rifle stretched straight ahead with his eye staring down the barrel. George Stone was ready to defend himself from any aggressor. Luckily for Stone, there was not one … at least in the immediate hills in front of him.

George Stone had landed on the side of a small mountain in the pitch dark and had no idea where he was. He felt numb not only from the cold that had taken a toll on his body but also from the tragedy and immense loss he had suffered several hours before. It was now finally daylight, and George had spent the last several hours hiding under a makeshift tent that was covered by snow. Right after he landed, George took his parachute and covered it with snow to hide it from the world or at least from anyone who might be looking for him. He then wrapped himself in his warmest clothing and buried himself in the snow under the white, flake-covered parachute. It was ingenious! The parachute covered up even the footprints he'd made in the snow. His hope was to be able to make it through the night unnoticed. He accomplished his goal. In fact, in the darkness no one noticed his solo parachute falling from the sky. The explosions around the plane lit up the sky, but he was far past the plane by the time it actually exploded. The previous night's lightshow was a good diversion for Stone as he floated down from the sky.

George stood up, crept out from under his snow-covered home and began to look around. If anyone had seen him drop into the hills and trees, surely they would have paid a visit by now. George would have heard them from his hiding spot, although they would not have seen him. Stone was successful at easing his troubled mind and was now comfortable that he was alone in the mountain woods. He convinced himself it was now safe for travel. George wanted to get as close to the crash site as possible to see if there were any survivors. Only thing … the wreck was on the other side of the mountain—to his best guess, at least five miles away—and it would surely be swarming with enemy activity. Still, George had to do whatever he could to check on his friends and especially his best friend Dale. He was positive that Dale had not survived the crash, but he needed confirmation. The blowing wind and hard weather would not allow for easy travel, but it would act as a nice cover. After being out in the weather for most of the night with nothing more than his coat and a parachute for warmth, George was getting a bit of frostbite. He knew that he did not have a lot of time to track down the wreckage and to find shelter for the night.

George reached down and slowly rolled his parachute into a small roll that looked like a sleeping bag. *It's amazing how something so big can wrap up into something so small,* he thought while rolling the lifesaving material. He was quick to dust off the snow from the parachute as he rolled it up to keep it dry, as any snow he let inside the parachute would make for a cold blanket. George then tied the chute to his backpack and tossed it over his shoulder. He also reached into his pocket and quickly counted his ammo.

"Thirty-six shells, two complete full hammers, and a couple of grenades," George counted softly. That's all George had to defend himself from the German army that lay somewhere down below the mountain.

George put his ammo back in the bag and tightened up his belt. He wiped his face to knock some of the frost that had gathered around his eyes off his face. He looked up at the mountain and knew the road ahead was a long one, but it was a journey he had to take. It seemed odd to George that he was in a constant state of fear right now, because as he looked around, all he could see was beauty. He was on the side of a small mountain range and standing in a group of trees. As he looked around, all he could see was peace. A smile encroached his face as off in the distance he saw two skinny pine trees next to each other about twenty feet apart. One of the branches was covered in snow and the weight of the moisture had forced it to drop and dangle a bit. George instantly thought it looked like football goal posts from his youth. The view made him smile because the trees appeared to open a clearing down the mountain, and it was as if George was looking through the two trees and off some twenty miles.

"I'd like to kick a football through that opening!" George said softly, joking to himself. The distant view was a nice one; nothing but green- and yellow-topped trees covered in snow. The snow also appeared to make walking paths down the mountain. George would have liked to jump right on those paths and head down, but he was not sure what he would encounter at the bottom. Unsure of what was at the end of the path, George decided he should avoid it. Also, according to his calculations, he was on the other side of the mountain from where the crash had occurred. The plane went down no less than five miles northeast of where he was. The quickest way to get there was probably over the small mountain, then back down the other side. George was doing all he could to take his mind off his situation. While he remained cautious, he was also trying to convince himself that the men who shot at his plane were not sitting somewhere up in these hills waiting for him to make an appearance.

He looked up at the solid gray sky. *The sun will not be coming out today!* He thought and then began his journey up the mountain, walking northeast.

NIGHTFALL

It took most of the day, but George finally made it over the snow-covered mountain and down through the thick winter brush to the crash site. He was several hundred feet above the wreckage but could tell there was enemy activity going on below. He reached into his backpack and pulled out his army issue small, black Bushnell binoculars. He pulled them to his eyes, squinted into them, and looked down at the site. The powerful lenses drew Stone closer to the site still in frenzy and under deep investigation. It was starting to get dark, and it looked like the several dozen Germen soldiers who were inspecting the site were about to leave. Most were headed to the trucks and carried items from the plane. George could not get close enough to see what the items were.

He closely examined the site from his mountain perch but could not tell if anyone survived the horrible ordeal. The crash site was surprisingly isolated, as if the plane had gone down nose first. Only a few hundred yards appeared to be burned by the crash. The area hit had suffered grave damage. Most of the trees in the area were blackened to the core, some still burning in small patches around the area. Smoke was the most dominant feature of the landscape; the gray and black fumes seemed to tail off for miles. These fumes had acted as a guide to George and enabled him to find the site so quickly. Although he was several hundred feet away and hidden behind a log, he could tell the movement at this site was not friendly. He was positive that no one had survived the crash except him. He was saddened but did not let that sadness overtake the thoughts that were in his head. George continued to look intently as he noticed the Germans starting to load some parts of the American plane into their truck. It was simple; there were no survivors. If someone had survived, the Germans would have finished him off by now.

George began to feel sad again and frustrated in many ways. It was clear that he was on his own. He had no idea where he was or where he was going. He'd had no communication with anyone, and anyone who might be looking for him probably thought he was dead. This was truly a fruitless mission for George, but he knew there was a reason he had survived. He pulled the lenses down from his eyes, wiped away some of the tears on them, and wrapped the binoculars in his homemade parachute backpack.

"There must be a reason my life was spared," George said to his God, who he believed must have been with him that day. "How did I get out?" There was no answer.

Stone knew he had to find shelter or he would surely die up here in the hills. George had to make this gift he was given count. This began his motivation. Right now this mountain belonged to him. He was going to have to find a way to live at least in the short term on this mountain. He would have to find a way to live here until he could figure out a way to escape this occupied area. He slowly reached down and grabbed some clean snow with his exposed hand. His fingers were so cold they had turned candy apple red. He picked up a handful of the snow and put it in his mouth. He could taste the dirt in the snow, but it mattered little, as he was dehydrated and needed some source of refreshment in his body. He still had some of the dried beef in his backpack but was saving that as long as he could. Besides, it made him even thirstier, and he had not found any clean water up to that point.

He looked down toward the crash site again and noticed that most of the troops were leaving, but others continued to search the area. He would not be able to conduct his own investigation until they left. Now his top priority was to find shelter.

George rolled over to his knees and slowly and quietly crawled back into the woods, trying to stay as low to the ground as possible. He had to be extra careful, as the enemy might have binoculars and could notice his movement in the woods. He slowly crawled away from the opening in which he had just been looking, so as to not be seen, and then vanished into the trees. When he was safely in the rough, he stood up and started walking. He decided to head north … but not the direction of his compass, instead by the altitude of the mountain. The higher he was the safer he was, and while it was a lot colder, that was better than the alternative

THE NEXT DAY

Another cold and windy night had gone by, and George was getting closer to becoming a frozen icicle. The previous night he had slept between a couple of downed trees, wrapped in the parachute. He also had a feeling of hunger that he had not felt in some time. It was a feeling that was tearing at his stomach so much that he was starting to feel light-headed and nauseated. Stone was searching for food along the way but knew he could not use his rifle, as the enemy soldiers patrolling below might hear the gunshot. If George could climb another five hundred feet or so, he could probably use his gun to shoot a rabbit or some other wildlife. Survival out here was a little tougher than he thought it would be. He had hunted before, but he did not consider himself a hunter. He knew how to use his gun but had never fired it in live action. His qualifications did not seem to fit the job requirements he had suddenly been thrust into as a soldier.

The sky was just as overcast as ever, and Stone had a pretty good idea snow would soon be falling again. Still, he forged ahead in the hard mountain snow, thinking shelter could not be far off. *A cave would be really nice right about now!* George suggested to himself.

As the young, wet, freezing soldier pressed on and continued to climb closer to the sky, he got a break. Just barely in his eyesight, he noticed a small white-tailed rabbit sitting back behind a row of snow-covered bushes. George knew this could be dinner and froze in his tracks. He had several matches in his bag, and dinner would be easy to cook and eat, even out here in the bitter cold. He was trying to save as many matches as he could for as long as possible because he knew he might be up here for a while, and he would need the heat of the fire to survive. George quietly dropped to his knees and set the end of his rifle in the edge of a tree stump, using the tree as a tri-pod to steady his shot. He rolled the eye site spec to the front of the rifle and then moved his head until his right eye could easily glare through it. He slowly lined up the rabbit and made sure the small bunny was perfectly in his target. He made sure he had his future dinner in site before he ever took the shot. With the noise of the rifle, he really only had one chance to get a shot off and not be located if anyone heard it.

His steady finger slowly slid down to the trigger, and he began to smile. He knew he was about to take the perfect shot that would provide him with a meal he had craved for some time. He no longer concerned himself with the noise from the shot because he was now sure no one below him would hear it, or maybe that was his hunger talking to him. He was not sure, but his mind was made up. If people did hear it, they would think it was coming from the other side of the mountain, or the shot would too far off for them to correctly locate. At least that's the story that George continued to repeat in his head. However, his hungry stomach was doing most of the thinking. It really did not matter if he was up in the mountains or down in the small town; he was starving, and he was going to shoot.

Pow! The rifle shot out, and the small, gray; furry rabbit fell backward at a massive speed. It was a perfect hit. George had dinner. He smiled, proud of his kill, and then stood up and softly ran in the heavy snow over to the rabbit. It was about a hundred-yard sprint, but that did not matter right now. George was as hungry as he could ever remember being in his life. He ran up to his prized possession, reached down, and picked it up. Dinner was not that far off. The rabbit was motionless, and the blood continued to run from the animal's neck. George looked around for a place to cook his dinner and then noticed something small and brown in the distance. George could not see it very well through the trees. To get a better view, he slowly moved forward toward the brown object, entering the mysterious backwoods forest. As he slowly walked through the woods, he raised his rifle in his right hand while holding the rabbit in his left hand. George stopped and then dropped to his feet, trying to hide ... it was a cabin. *Was someone inside? Did he hear the gunshot?* George did not know.

He had fired his gun, and there was no hiding that. If people were in the cabin, they would surely have come out by now. It was getting darker, but in caution, George poked his head up from behind a dirt-covered log that was his cover. As his helmet overtook the top of the log, his deep blue eyes quickly panned the small cabin. He could see a trace of steam or smoke coming out the top of the chimney, but there was no light, no flame to give away vacancy. The smoke also appeared to be a slight stream, as if a fire had burned but extinguished long ago, maybe as long as a day or two. George sat upright and dropped his rabbit next to him as he moved both hands to the rifle in a ready position. He continued to stare at the cabin and desperately searched the grounds in front of him, expecting a live body to come out of the cabin at any time. George could feel the numbness of his feet. He thought to himself that where there was smoke there was a fire, and if no one was inside, that was where George could spend the night. *Besides I am miles away from anyone. If someone does live there, I will have the element of surprise.* It was a plan made in haste but nonetheless a good plan.

The cabin was very small. From the outside it did not look like more than a room or two and what appeared to be a window from a loft upstairs.

So it must be two levels, he thought. It was also very old looking. It was a true 1800s log cabin, and that made George a little more interested in it. The sidewalls were almost gray from old age, and the roof was white, covered in snow. There was a small step up to the front door that greeted visitors as they approached. As far as George could tell from his angle, there were no other doors in or out of the cabin unless there was one on the backside. The ends of the walls were like ladders, as every other log poked out from the side up to the roof. There were a couple of long, skinny trees that surrounded the old cabin, but for the most part the land around it was open and exposed. It was as if someone had cleared a small patch out of these woods several years ago and built this log cabin. George did not know if it was the cold weather, his stomach, or just the allure of the newly discovered shelter, but he suddenly found himself walking closer and closer to it. He was careful as he slipped from behind one tree to another.

George realized that he had forgotten the rabbit and quickly returned to it. He reached back down, grabbed his dinner, and then stood upright and in a ready position. The small cabin was about a hundred yards away, and the overcast sky was fleeing quickly. George looked around and reexamined his approach to the small cabin. He moved cautiously toward it, slowly yet swiftly and looking from side to side. He moved from tree to tree, rifle in one hand, rabbit in the other, with his head moving in all directions looking for any signs of life. More importantly, George also checked the snow looking for any kind of footprints, but he did not see any. *Could this good fortune be mine? Could I have actually stumbled across a place for warmth, yet also a place hidden so far away from the world?* He wondered. He was an American soldier somewhere behind enemy lines, and he was actually about to find refuge in a cabin far away from civilization. *Could this be for real? Could I actually be this lucky?* He questioned himself continually.

George moved within a few steps of the rustic wood door, and still no signs of life came from inside the cabin. Surely if someone was watching him he would have been shot by now. He approached the side of the cabin and slid down along the window. His head slowly rose to the window seal to look inside. He peeked in. The room was dark and had a cold feel to it, but no one, as far as George could see, was inside. He moved closer to the front door. He looked down and noticed what appeared to be smaller footprints, maybe those of a child or a small woman. It was obvious the prints did not belong to a man. George continued to look around for other prints but did not see any that caused alarm to the recently trained soldier. The smaller footprints trailed off into the woods, and he was not sure where they headed after that. The door was closed, so George used his left hand that was holding the rabbit and turned the knob slowly. He looked down and noticed the rabbit left a blood trail nearly all the way from the woods right up to the front door of the cabin he was about to open.

"Shit!" he blurted out. George knew that anyone returning to the cabin would surely see the blood, and his advantage of surprise would be lost. He shrugged his head in disgust and began to work on the doorknob again. He turned the rust-colored knob to the right and could hear the lock inside clicking as it opened. The door was not locked. George used his rifle to push the door open the rest of the way. The large, old door made a loud creak as George entered the home. With every step he took the floor would make another creek. It was as if the cabin was sending a warning to anyone inside he had entered the home. George looked around, but there were no recent signs of life. The room was very cold as he looked around and noticed the smoldering wood that was in the fireplace. There had been life in here sometime in the last couple of days, but for some reason that life had moved on and not returned.

George was not sure he really wanted to light a fire, but he was cold and he needed to eat, so he had no choice. His plan was to keep his rifle close by his side at all times. Maybe he would just get lucky and whoever lived here would not return anytime soon. George quickly realized just how lucky he'd been the last forty-eight hours. He was the only one to make it out of the plane alive, and he had now found this wonderful shelter. He did not want to think about the crash—at least not right now. This cabin was a dream come true and maybe the first real break he'd been blessed with since he stepped on the train with Dale back in White City several months earlier. But right now his most important job was to start a fire, warm his fingers, and cook his dinner.

George set the rabbit down on the table in front of him and laid his rifle next to it. He walked over to the fireplace and grabbed three small logs from the tray next to the hard rock structure. He tossed the logs in the fireplace and then reached into his pocket and pulled out a box of matches. He took his blisteringly cold, red, and chafed fingers and struck the match on the box, protecting the flame as he lowered the match to the logs. George softly blew on the flame as it connected with the timber, and a solid flame began to grow in the fireplace. George smiled as he instantly felt the warmth take over his body. It felt good. He could feel his face start to tingle from the sweet, warm rays that were coming out of the fire. It felt as if he was still sitting by the fire of his Kansas farm home several thousand miles away. He cherished the memories of his family and longed to be back home. He rubbed his hands and put them close to the fire and was anxiously waiting to pull off his boots and warm his toes. As the fire popped, he quickly thought of his rifle and turned to it. The rifle and the rabbit lay on the table where he had put them.

He didn't seem as hungry right now as he had been just a few minutes before, but another part of his body was eating right now, and it sure felt good.

The glow of the fire lit the room, and George could make out more of the furniture and supplies this cabin was now allowing to him. He could also see there was a loft for a bedroom that he had noticed from outside. He leaned back up from the fire and walked over to pick up his rifle. The young, solo soldier moved slowly to the ladder that led to the loft and began to climb it. The old wood from the ladder cracked under his weight as he went from step to step. George had to make sure no one was hiding up there, and the cabin was clear for him to relax, and more importantly, to get to work on his dinner.

Leading with his rifle, he peeked over the top of the loft. The soft fire glow that spread to the loft was enough illumination for George to make out a bed that was surprisingly neatly made yet no one was in that small room either. George stepped back down the ladder and moved toward the table. He knew his fire would not last long and that he would have to soon get more wood. He grabbed the rabbit and put it in a bowl that was on the table. His dinner was still leaking blood, and it had drained a nice little puddle on the table. George grabbed his collar on both sides and pulled it up tight. He walked over to the door, rifle in hand, opened it, and looked around in caution one more time. As he looked, he noticed it was a little darker than before, but there was still no sign of anyone. There was not even a noise or a pop from the woods. It seemed unusually silent on this evening. George needed to find some wood, so he stepped back outside the cabin.

Why not follow the footprints? George thought.

He pulled the door shut and followed the small footprints as they led him into the woods. He had not been in the house for more than twenty minutes, but the darkness was intense. George squinted his eyes a bit but desperately went to work looking for tree limbs and sticks or any kind of wood that would get him through the night. There was plenty of it. With nearly every step he took there were little logs and twigs for him to pick up. It was if someone chopped the logs a long time ago and left them laying all around for him to find. George picked up the spare pieces and shook the snow off of them. He filled his arms and walked around to the backside of the cabin. He repeated this behavior another three times: picking up the wood, shaking off the snow, and then shoving the wood under his left arm. All he needed now were bigger pieces that would last while he slept. In an effort to locate larger logs, he walked a little farther into the woods. The smaller footprints disappeared in another direction, but he no longer needed them to guide him back to the cabin; he knew his way.

As he searched and searched for larger logs, he saw something that caught his attention. It was something that appeared to be a log standing on its side. But it was dark, and he could not make out what it was. He walked in that direction, all the while staring at the object, trying to decide out what it was, while carrying the three larger logs he had found under his left arm. As he got closer to the curiously shaped log, he raised his rifle in his right hand. With three logs under one arm and his rifle in the other, George crept closer to the object.

To his sudden shock, the object was not a log at all—it was a shoe ... a shoe that was connected to a body. The body was that of a young woman. George dropped his firewood and quickly fell to his knees. The woman was pale, and he could not tell if she was dead or alive. She was fully clothed in a heavy winter jacket and what appeared to be a homemade wool dress and heavy black boots. The woman had dark brown, almost black, hair, but it was partially drowned in the white snow. Her eyes were closed, and it was evident that she had been there for some time. It was also clear to George that she was the source of the small footprints in the snow and was probably the occupant of the cabin that George was now calling his home.

He bent down to her and put his cold hand on her even colder neck ... there was a slight pulse. George dropped his rifle and wiped the snow off the mysterious body. As he wiped, he noticed that her other boot was clamped down in a rusted rabbit trap. George could tell she experienced a ton of pain. The sharp teeth of the trap had cut into her ankle, and blood was beginning to freeze around her lower leg. The wind picked up as the night grew darker. George reached down and struggled to free her foot from the jaws that clamped to her. He managed to pull both sides away and lift her foot from the trap. The dried blood from her ankle stuck to the trap, and George knew this was a bad sign. He tossed the closed trap aside and rubbed the woman's face to give her warmth, but there was no response.

He took his rifle and worked it through the belt that was around his waist, leaned over, bent down on one knee, and picked up the woman. He held her in his arms. One arm around her neck, his other arm under her knees, he carried her back the long distance to the cabin. For now the young rescuer had lost his hunger for the rabbit. His hunger was now aimed in a third direction. He scampered his way back through the heavy snow, knowing that he would soon return for the wood. His feet kicked snow up with every thrust, but he did not feel the cold, bitter sting. His mind refocused one more time.

Part 3

DOVER, ENGLAND
1937

These are the scenes that poets write about. The daily beauty that is all around us goes unnoticed if no one is paying attention. These thoughts rolled through Richard Wild's head as he softly guided his mount through the lush English prairie land. He still had a hard time driving his automobile. He preferred to travel by horseback; it was more relaxing and quiet. Hearing the little sounds meant the world to Wild.

Off to his right was a field of yellow. Millions of bright sunflowers had collected in a single spot. The deep yellow petals circled the orange and brown inner layer … one after another. It had to extend beyond a country mile. A distant homestead sat quietly in the middle of the field, although it appeared to be vacant. Maybe the family was forced off their land. That was a common occurrence these days. Maybe the dust of the years caused this family to leave and abandon their home that would later turn so beautiful. *It's a shame the family is not around to view the beauty of this magnificent land,* Wild told himself.

The yellow horizon was also home to gray and blue. The sky was as blue as Richard had ever seen it. In the distance, the gray clouds were collecting, trying to build steam. Soon the gray would overtake the blue, causing this surreal picture to change. Richard knew he had time to enjoy the scenery because the rain was still several hours away, if it would fall at all on him. That's the good thing about the country. It was big, and not everything or every situation affected everyone in it. Richard was a county keeper of the peace, not really a lawman and not quite a criminal. He was on his way north to talk to a man he had never met. This man was currently in jail and requested that Richard come see him. Why would a prisoner he had never met request an audience with him? It did not make sense, but Richard agreed to the meeting. He was not the person who arrested him or had done his family wrong in any way. *Why is this particular inmate so interested in me?* The part-time lawman pondered these questions as he made the eighty-nine-mile trip.

The scenery was a welcome distraction and a chance for his mind to take a break from the questions surrounding this bizarre request.

Richard and his brown-and-white-spotted mount rode upon another vacant ranch. They continued on by the old homestead but took a brief moment to examine the fence that lined the property. He noticed the wood log railing that was stacked along with a solid single post. The posts were buried every so many feet, and the logs were simply placed in the groves of the wood, each overlapping the next posts. He also noticed that the barbwire had long since rusted but lined the wood and made a wonderful protective cover to keep out unwanted visitors. *The design is a good one and must have been built by a military mind.* Wild was in awe of the construction.

The wars on these fronts were many, and maybe this was why the sturdy fence was built. The ranch was vacant and the grass was high, but the home and the barn were still standing. *The fence must have done its job*, Richard thought.

Still, the road north was a lonely one for a single rider, and his mind wandered back to the mysterious inmate he would soon meet. While he tried to stay off topic by talking to and petting his horse, his mind really had one focus … the business up north.

THE NEXT DAY

It was nothing more than a wooden cell. In fact, the walls appeared to be eaten by insects and would fall apart at even the slightest touch. Still, this was a jail, and many called it home. Richard had no idea why he had been summoned to the dirty, smelly dungeon that was shaped like an old English fort. However, he knew he would not be there long.

The handle was wrought iron but had flakes of rust that fell off in his hand as he opened the door. The large wooden seal made unusual creaks and churned as it slid open. Inside was a small walkway. On each side of the dark path sat two jail cells, four in all. As Wild walked into the cell, the guard behind him raised his voice.

"Hold up," said the guard in a familiar English accent. "I need your pistols. You can't go in there with your silver."

Richard turned to the guard and reached down to his belt. He undid the brass buckle and pulled the holster around his body and then handed it over to the guard.

"It'll be out here when you've finished." He paused. "Eaton's in the last cell on the left."

Richard turned and walked slowly down the dark path lined by the metal bars on each side. It was actually only ten or more steps, but with each step he could hear the crack of the wood underneath his boots. The smell was something Wild expected. It was emanating from the pans used as toilets in this small building. The first cell on the left was empty, as was the cell on the right. He noticed the beds were in perfect order, as if they lay waiting for their next occupant. The cells did have a prison feel to them. The bars lined the front of the cells, and they ran the distance of the room on both sides and up to the ceiling on top. They were not very big and were separated by a single row of wrought iron down the middle. Richard could not see the face of the man in the first cell; his back was to the walk way as he lay horizontal on his bed. The instant odor from the room almost choked Wild at first, but he was slowly getting used to it.

As he approached the second jail cell on the right, he noticed a chair lying against the wall outside the cell. He looked in but only saw the legs of a man creeping out from a bottom bunk. The cell had a small window in the back also filled with iron, but the sun was shining brightly through it. The bright sun was helping to hide the face of the man in the cell, but Richard could see the prisoner was alone. Richard looked again, squinting his eyes a bit to see if he could see the man, but he could not. The room was silent until Wild forced out, "You Eaton?"

There was no reply. Richard stood there for a second longer. He began to use the brim of his hat to try and block the sun and catch a glimpse of the man.

"I say again ... you Eaton?" Richard said in a very authoritative voice.

"Why don't you sit down?" came a voice from under the bunk. "They went to all that trouble as to bring you a chair and all."

"I'll stand," Wild replied. "Don't plan to be here long."

The room again drew silent ... then ...

"I didn't either, but I guess I had no choice." The man started to move and slowly came into sight as he moved from under the bunk. He was wearing a black-and-white jail issue pant and shirt combination that was well worn and in dire need of a wash. As the man stood up and slowly began his five-step walk to the cell gate, his face came into focus. Richard quickly skimmed his face and tried to put it with a place in his memory, but he had no luck. The man was about the same height as Wild and had some of the same features, but he was not a man Wild recognized.

"What do you want with me?" Wild asked.

The man approached the end of the cell and reached over for his own chair. As the chair slid to him, Richard could see the shackles on his wrists and feet. The man smelled like a horse after a three-day ride, and his face did not fare well either. It was just as rough. He had a soft whisker beard and had sweat rolling from his forehead to his chin. His clothes appeared to be dripping from the sweat, and this made Richard realize just how scorching hot it was in the room. He reached up and pulled his collar to let out some steam and then did something that had become a Wild family trademark. He put a look on his face that was as serious as death and began to stare the man straight in the eyes. Richard had learned this move from his father, and it was something that usually achieved great success. The look could call a man out or call his bluff, and Wild would instantly be able to read him and understand him. Richard wanted to feel this man out; he wanted to find out just how far this man was willing to go. The man known as Jamie Eaton was just as serious and responded with his own little smirk that caught Wild off guard. It was as if the man was laughing in his own mind. He smiled in a strange way as his eyes rolled a little into his head. His tongue hung slightly out of his mouth as he appeared dizzy and made soft, sudden moves.

"You all right?" Wild asked.

"What I am is of no concern to you. Why don't you take a sit and we'll talk," Eaton scuffed. The man's breath was so bad Richard nearly had to look away as not to smell it as he talked some five feet and behind a row of metals bars away from Wild.

Richard, curious, reached over and grabbed the chair, turned it backward, and sat on the seat with his arms crossed on the back of the chair. Eaton struggled with the chains that continued to cling as he tried to sit down in the chair. He expressed obvious frustration as he dropped into the seat.

The two men stared intensely at each other.

"What do you want?" Wild asked.

The man rolled his tongue as if to lick his lips and leaned forward. "I got a d'ept to pay."

"A debt to who?" Wild replied while still trying to get used to the man's bad breath.

"I got a d'ept to pay and some redemption due me!" Eaton remarked.

Richard got a curious look. "What kind of debt?" he asked.

The man smiled. "The best kind."

"Why did you ask me to come here?" Wild cut in.

"You're the constable, right? The son of the great colonel, right?"

"Wild was my father," Richard declared vehemently.

"I got a d'ept to pay and redemption … due me!" Eaton commanded.

"You're too late, Eaton! The colonel was gunned down three years ago. There's no payback to get on him. The debt has been paid by someone else!"

"You're not listening to me. I don't care who I pay the d'ept to … I got a d'ept to pay and redemption due me," Eaton urged.

Richard sat quiet for a few seconds then offered these words to Eaton.

"If that's a threat and that's the best you can do, you've wasted my time," Richard exploded. "I eat and shit crap like you every day. You step one foot out of this cell, and I'd blow your head off!"

The room grew quiet for a few seconds, and then Eaton responded.

"Let me tell you a little story … a sonnet if you will or an anecdote, whatever you prefer." The man paused. "Two thousand nine hundred and twenty days. Let me say that again: two thousand … nine hundred," again he paused, "and twenty days. That's eight years. That's how long I've been in this cell. That's how long I've lived in this shit hole. Eight years I've been sleeping in that so-called bed. Eight years I been seeing men come in here and men get hanged. I can't tell you how many men—I lost count after six—but I'm pretty sure it's over a hundred." Eaton turned his head toward the man across the room in the other cell. "Pierce over there, he's next. Not sure when he hangs, but he'll hang."

Wild continued to sit quietly and stare at the man with his rough look.

"You want to know a secret? A small room can drive a man crazy. But here's the good news …" He leaned into Wild and started to whisper, "Crazy is good. Crazy will set you free."

Richard leaned back and started to shake his head.

"Eaton, you've been in here too long!"

"Two thousand … nine hundred and twenty days!" Eaton yelled at the top of his lungs. Then he was quiet again. "But here's the good news: crazy will set me free." He paused. "I got paroled." Eaton started to smile. "I'm out of here in thirty days. Thirty days and I'm a free man."

"Why does that interest me?" Wild asked.

Eaton answered softly, "I got a d'ept to pay and some redemption due me."

"Where are you looking to find that redemption?" Wild asked.

The man looked Richard right in the eyes. "Dover!"

Richard fell back from the chair and rose to his feet. "I'll kill you before you leave this jail cell, I swear I will."

"Dover will fall, and you will fall with it," Eaton explained. "In thirty days I'm a free man, and I'm coming to kill you!" boasted Eaton.

"Come see me in thirty days, and I'll do what my father was not able to do. I'll take you down. He may have put you behind bars, but Eaton, I'll put you in the dirt!" Wild said commandingly.

"Oh, he didn't put me here. In fact, I probably deserved this. What the great colonel did to my family will never be forgotten … or forgiven. If he's dead, that d'ept passes to his next of kin. It passes to you, and I will collect on it. You will die in thirty days in his name. And I will piss on your grave!"

Richard continued to get very angry but was able to hold his composure.

"I'll be waiting. I'll see you in thirty days. I'll be the one to truly set you free," Wild answered.

"I got a d'ept to pay … and you will pay!" Eaton shouted out.

Richard kicked the chair over and started walking back toward the large wooden door.

"I got a d'ept to pay … and you will pay! I got a d'ept to pay … and you will pay!" Eaton continued to shout out. "I got a d'ept to pay … and you will pay! I got a d'ept to pay … and you will pay … because, brother, I am your brother. The colonel was my father as well, and he pissed all over my kin. He left us to fend and left us to be shamed and forgotten. I'm here to say, I got a d'ept to pay … and you will pay!"

Richard walked up to the door and kicked it open. The door slammed against the outside wall, shocking the guard, and then the wrought-iron door slammed shut.

"I don't know who you are or what kind of shit you are trying to pull on me, but I'll be waiting! You bring that debt to me and you'll be in the dirt!" Richard yelled as he stormed down the short walkway. "Don't know what kind of man thinks he can talk that way about the colonel, but I know what I can do about it. You and I don't share the same blood! This cell has driven you crazy, but I'll be waiting for you in Dover, and we'll finish this. You got that, Eaton?"

Richard left the room.

"I got a d'ept to pay … and you will pay!" Eaton laughed so hard he started to cry. "I got a d'ept to pay … and you will pay!"

Hearing all the noise, the other prisoner rolled over in his bed and sat up. He wiped the sweat from his face and long gray beard. He turned to Eaton.

"I thought you get out in fifteen days?" the prisoner asked.

Eaton, still sitting in his chair, leaned forward and pushed his face as hard as he could between the bars. He smiled and his tongue rolled out of his month as his eyes rolled back into his head. He pulled his face back as two metal rust marks now lined his face. His greasy black hair was standing on end as he turned to the other inmate, Pierce, and softly said, "It's ten days actually!"

Flower Rainbow

Richard's wife, Nada, spent all morning out in the garden planting flowers. It was a hobby that helped make the Wild ranch one of the prettiest ranches in the region. Visitors to the ranch were at a minimum, so her long hours of hard work were rarely recognized or noticed, but she received great satisfaction from her laborious efforts. It was a hobby that added purpose to an otherwise uneventful day.

As Richard walked around the side of the barn, he looked out upon the rainbow of flowers that lined the southwest side of his land. The rows were perfect in nature, all standing in perfect uniform, like soldiers about to head to battle. Only this was a beautiful sight, a refreshing sight, and one that made Wild smile every time he walked around this side of the barn. Nada's efforts were not fruitless. Richard often wondered how she strategically lined the flowers so straight and so perfect. Three rows of red, two of yellow, three more of red, and a sprinkling of orange and purple. The view was a lot like her personality—regular at first, then the more you got to know her, the more complicated she became.

"Those are some beautiful flowers!" Richard said softly, although he knew Nada could not hear him; she was too far away.

Richard continued to walk around the front of the barn on a mission to find his daughter, Eve. He walked into the doorway of the ol' red barn and slid the door open all the way.

"Eve? You in here?" he asked. Wild was always concerned with the whereabouts of his young daughter. She was his pride and joy; she was his life. He would do whatever it took to keep her safe. It was easy to tell why he was so concerned when he could not find her.

Wild looked up as he heard a noise, and a young woman appeared from the top of the barn. The girl had been sliding back and forth on the pulley that was used to pull hay.

"Sir?" Eve offered to her quickly relieved father.

"Enough horse play. Come on down; we've got to finish the back fence."

The young woman, in her late teens, grabbed a handful of rope and dropped it down over the front of the barn. The pulley that she had been swinging from was now her transportation to the ground. Her father watched as the girl dropped down. She was either a tomboy or a very independent woman for her age. Despite her independent spirit, she was very quiet and shy. Many times in her life, her family and friends wondered if she was right in the head because she was so quiet. But that was just her personality—tough and strong, yet quiet. She was probably more like her father than he would have liked her to be.

"I swear you were born in a barn!" her father joked.

The two walked out of the barn and turned to walk along the stretch of fence that lined the back of the barn. The first several rows of fence were littered with several long wood boards running horizontal from post to post. All were four boards high and surrounded the barn, but as the two ranch hands walked farther, the long, thick horizontal boards turned into long wood logs. Each fence post was set top to bottom, and the logs ran the distance of the posts in the shape of a large W. From post to post ran barbwire, and this was the job Richard was hoping to complete with his daughter. It was an idea he'd gotten recently on the trip north, and it was that trip now warning him to add some barbwire to the fence.

"Why do we need all this barbwire? You haven't seen a coyote, have you, Father?" asked Eve as she picked up a post of the metal fencing.

"Sometime coyotes aren't the only killers to worry about," her father replied.

The two walked up and grabbed the tools they had left laying from the day before.

"Grab the wire and hold it up as I work it through the wood," Richard ordered. Eve reached around to her back pocket and pulled out an old pair of gloves that were way too big for her. She threaded them on her fingers and then picked up the wire.

"What killers are coming?" she murmured oddly.

Richard paused in amazement. He could not believe how clever his only child had become.

"Here's the thing about killers: anything and anyone can be a killer if you let them," he replied.

"I'm not scared!" she declared indignantly.

The two continued to work. Eve held the rigid wire while Richard hammered it into the wood.

"This line of work is not for everybody, Eve. You deal with some bad people ... people who don't care about rules." He paused. "People who make their own rules! People who are better off dead than alive; that's the way I see it. Sometimes you have to give them what they are asking for."

"You ever shoot a man, Father? I mean ... shoot him dead?"

"Yes, I have, Eve. I didn't really want to, but I had to. Otherwise I might already be buried in the dirt."

"What did he do that made you want to shoot him?"

"Well, there have been several. It's just the job that I have. It's my job to protect people from the bad men. I suppose they didn't do anything to me. I'd never met the man till he pulled his silver. Then I shot him dead.

"Why all the questions? You know what I do; you know what your grandfather did. Our job is to keep the peace and take down anyone who tries to change that."

Richard hammered a little bit longer and then dropped down to one knee and set the hammer on the ground.

"Eve, in life there's just one way ... the right way. Some people don't see it that way and turn bad."

"What makes them turn bad?"

Wild looked down and then back up to his daughter. He raised his arm and put his hand on her shoulder with fatherly compassion.

"Sometimes people get all riled up in their soul. Their mind wanders, and they let the moment get out of hand. They lose control, and anything can happen. Funny thing is, all we got is control. That's what separates the good from the bad ... control. It's what turns normal people into heroes and villains into wild dogs. Wild dogs got no control; they can't help what their instincts tell them to do."

"So you kill men when they go wild?"

"I don't kill anyone, 'less it's to defend myself, my family, or my county. I don't kill anyone who's not looking to be killed."

He paused and then put his hand over on the fence.

"That's why we build strong fences: to keep the wild dogs out. Sure, they could jump over the fence, but it serves as one last warning. Take a step back, mister ... think about your actions before you proceed. Think about control and who will be in control if you go over this fence. A wild dog may not see that or understand it, but a man will. When he makes that choice to go over the fence, he'll know what he's getting into. And we'll know what kind of man we're dealing with. That's where I come in. That's my job."

Richard grabbed his hammer and pulled back up to his feet. He pulled on the wire and began hammering more barbwire.

"Eve, people are not any better than other people. Don't ever hate someone 'cause of the way they were born. People are different, and in the end that's what makes everyone the same: the fact that we're all different. It's what we become and what we pass on to our children that judge a man or a woman. Some choose to do what's right ... make living pleasurable for everyone. Others choose to force their suffering on other people—good people. My father taught me to not let that happen. I never wanted to be a keeper of the peace until the day I saw him die. That's the day I learned about control. That was my father's final lesson for me."

"Aren't you scared of dying, Father? Aren't you scared of dying the way he did?"

"Being scared is no fun. Besides, I got no time to worry about fear. I got a fence to finish."

Eve smiled as the two continued to work away on the fence. The young woman looked up at the clouds around the ranch.

"I love you, Father!" she told him.

"I love you too, Eve." Wild looked down at his hands and pulled off a glove. His concern for his daughter had just gotten the best of him.

"Listen, Eve?" Wild offered in a somewhat softer voice than before. "Your grandfather was raised just across the channel in France. He's from the town of Calais. It's just straight across the channel, maybe two hours in a small boat. His boyhood home is there. It's about five miles straight northeast of the town … up a mountain."

The young woman looked at her father with even more concern than before.

"Up the mountain is a small wooden shack not much bigger than our barn, but it's a good home, a safe home. I want you to remember this, okay?" Eve nodded. "I want you to remember this place. If anything ever happens to me, I want you to take Nada and get across the channel to Calais. I want you to find that cabin and stay there, okay? We live in a very dangerous time. Your grandfather and I did things that some people did not take kindly to and may try to take out their revenge on us. Do you understand?"

"Yes, Father. I will try and find the cabin if I need to," Eve replied.

"Good. It's a safe place. You can stay there as long as you need to. I hope you never have to, but sometimes I worry about what lies ahead. I worry the future will bring bad days instead of good ones. I worry that what we have built might soon be destroyed. I see that day coming," Richard warned.

"Father, you scare me. But I'll do whatever you need me to do," Eve responded.

"I know you will," Richard said confidently.

The two continued to work on the fence.

THE WAITING

"So how are we going do this?" asked Nathan Christner, the local constable, sitting across from Richard Wild in the newly constructed Dover Law office. The room was large, and the walls were fresh. The jail cells were so new that they had few occupants and had not yet succumbed to the common jailhouse stink. This office was more like a nice teahouse than a detention center, and Nathan intended to keep it that way. That's what made today's meeting so important.

The two men gathered in the late afternoon hour to discuss their plan to stop the man who was coming to try and kill Wild in just over twenty days. Christner was a young lawman good looking, confident, but not long in experience with these types of situations. His beliefs were shared by Wild, and the young man cared more about the town than most of the lady callers who showed up at his office door with petty jobs for the young constable.

It was not unusual for Nathan to sit in his office sipping a cup of tea or eating a piece of home-baked pie rather than arresting someone. Nathan was a soft, gentle man with a squared-off jaw that made him the talk of the town. His light brown hair cast over his inset eyes. His impressive looks made him the town bachelor that most young women hoped to impress. He was a well-educated man and believed in the new school of law enforcement rather than the shoot 'em up old style. Nathan could talk, but it was his tender voice more than his youthful experience that earned him the job. Was he too young for such a position? Probably, and he knew it, but it was a job he felt he could grow into. He wasn't the best shot with the gun, but when it came to talking out problems, he was a natural. That was his new religion for law, talk first, and shoot later. So it was not out of the norm that today he was in his office holding a cup filled with hot tea and talking to Richard Wild to try and solve this complex problem.

Christner was sitting in the soft chair that was usually where convicts sat, but during slow times, Nathan liked to make it his own. Richard, on the other hand, was pacing back and forth in front of his desk. With every turn the cracks in the floor were expressing his concerns more that Wild ever could.

"The man is a killer, and I'm not sure why they are letting him out! But if he comes here looking for me, I'll drop him. I just need to find a way to make sure my family is safe."

Wild stopped pacing and slammed his hand down on the desk sitting in the office.

"Dover used to be a mean territory, full of killers, but now it's different. I've tried to make this place a safe town for everybody. No vagrant is coming to my town to change that." He paused. "I don't understand the violence; I don't understand the hate. Some people live to kill; others have to kill to live. Death is too permanent, Nathan. I got too many things to do before I die."

He paused again, and Nathan could tell by the tone of his voice, Wild was unsure of himself. Wild continued, "The blood killers! People try to justify what they've done by comparing themselves to others. Make other folks feel like they deserved it. But old men are wise. We know the errors of our ways and the consequences of our actions. That's part of the aging process. We know hate don't do any man good. But it don't fall off, that much hate. That much hate doesn't go away. That much hate becomes dangerous and makes a man crazy. A crazy man doesn't care for nothing or no one. Only cure for a man with that much hate … a bullet. Understand?"

Nathan leaned up to the desk in front of the men and sat his cup of tea down onto it, making sure not to spill any on the new wooden desk.

"I understand, Wild, but every man gets a fair shake until proven otherwise. I can't stop a man who hasn't done anything. It's just not my way," Nathan exclaimed.

"We have to protect the citizens; we have to protect the people. We are the law, and the laws are how we live. There's just no room in this life for men who don't respect them," Wild tossed back. Richard reached over and picked up his rifle that was sitting by the door.

"Men are scared by nature, and they think they will find their answers in the barrel of a gun." He held it up. "But after a while they forget the questions and live by the rules of the gun. They think those rules will lead them far away from those that scared 'em. They think the mighty rifle will lead them to paradise, but it's the road through purgatory they end up on. Every man has his point—a point where he's afraid to go yet he keeps trying to get there. Finally he pushes that point. Hell, he didn't want to be there anyway. Killin' … don't make any man better. It just makes him weak and dependent. It's a place no man should ever have to go." Wild cocked the rifle open and looked down the empty barrel. He then slammed it shut and set the rifle back down on the table. Richard had said his piece and was now a bit more reserved. Nathan crossed his arms and leaned back in his well-relaxed chair.

"Nathan, Eaton says he's my brother or at least my half brother. He says the colonel done him wrong a long time ago. I just don't know what to think of that." The young constable reached over, carefully picked up his hot tea, and then took a sip. He leaned his chair back and kicked his legs up onto the table. His boots were black, and they were as shiny as his unused side arm that was in the holster around his waist. "People make mistakes every day. They will today, and they will tomorrow. Why should yesterday be any different?"

"You can count on me, Wild. I'll be here when you need me. We'll keep peace in this town. I just ask that we make sure that what we are doing is the right thing. I want to have a chance to talk to Eaton before anyone makes a move. You okay with that?"

Richard shook his head in agreement but showed concern as he picked up his rifle and reached for the doorknob.

"I don't want charges coming down on me if I have to handle this. Understood?" he asked in a stronger tone toward Christner.

"I understand. Heck I'll be right there next to you if need be. Here in the next couple of weeks I'll wire for some help just to be safe. By the time Eaton gets to Dover, we'll have a town full of lawmen. You can count on that," Christner answered back in confidence.

Richard Wild shook his head, opened the door, and walked out of the office. The skinny wooden door slammed behind him. Christner sat his cup back down and pulled his revolver out of its holster. He opened the barrel and spun the empty chamber a couple of times before closing it. After this playtime with his weapon, he slid the handgun back into its permanent home.

Unexpected Visitor

The clutter of the hooves finally came to a stop as Richard Wild hopped off the back of his mount and walked toward the saloon. On a normal day he would not have been in the mood for a drink, but for some reason this tavern was calling him. Richard was not one to commonly hit the bottle, but today he felt like dropping one back before he headed back into the street.

He stepped up the walk and headed inside the saloon.

He could have been the son of just about anyone: a storekeeper, a blacksmith, a farmer, or maybe even a drifter. Either way life would have been a little easier for Richard Wild, at least to this point and especially on this day. But Richard was the son of the most honored man in the territory and maybe the Eastern Shore. Colonel Washington Wild could have been a knight if he had put his mind to it. The people loved and adored him. He was a glorified war hero who turned constable and became the most trusted man in the state. Only thing was the colonel had a side that few saw. Between the nightmares of war, the cold sweats of the bottle, and the longing guilt of a hidden love, the Colonel was fighting his own private battle. It was a battle he had long since lost, and unknown to most, he'd become corrupt. The hero did many wrongs that could never be righted, and since this discovery, his son Richard had begun his own battle. His trusted father became more devious than most of the men he was putting behind bars. He took money to arrest innocent men, and he killed for gold on more than one occasion. His legacy was in ruins, but only a handful of people knew this, and the colonel had taken care of them one by one.

Despite his poor morals, the colonel could not force himself to take the life of his first son, a boy named Eaton. He'd fathered the child sometime before with a woman he knew very little about. He tried to disown the boy but could never totally remove himself from his son's life. He even allowed his first son to travel with him from time to time, exposing him to the parts of his life he wanted most to forget. When the colonel became bored with this piece of his life, he framed the boy and sent him to prison. Many years later Eaton escaped and joined a gang. He became a killer. He had one ambition—to kill his father. Before he was able to accomplish his lifelong goal, he was recaptured and returned to jail. His worst day was when he discovered the colonel had been shot and that it was not by his own hands. The bullet did not come from his gun, and he would always have to live with that regret. However, Eaton received news of a half brother from another inmate. This news revived his lust for life and his lust for revenge against the father who never wanted him.

As for Richard, he was there the day his father was gunned down. The young man watched as his father dropped to the cold, hard ground in instant death ... he was the one who had pulled the trigger. Richard felt helpless that day and figured it was something he owed to his father—a bullet in the back from his son. Richard vowed to continue his father's good work as a lawman; all along knowing the family bloodline had a dark side. Now he too had a secret. Long ago he'd stumbled onto his father's activities. Richard made it his life's goal to cover up the negative side of his father and make his legacy a long lasting one—a legacy the town of Dover would be proud of. Richard refused to wear a badge. He refused to put on a piece of metal that would send out the wrong message, and his message was clear ... clean up the town and keep it that way. However, his hidden agenda was to protect his father's past and create an enigma that would make his family and this town beam with pride.

But today all that was about to catch up to Richard Wild. All the horrors of his father's secret life were on the line, and he was the one set to suffer the consequences. Richard was about to face the greatest challenge of his life. If he failed, the town and everything he had worked for the last two decades would collapse. For this, Wild thought it was okay to oblige in a drink.

Sundown was always Richard's favorite part of the day. It usually meant his work was over and he could retire to his family. But on this hot afternoon the greatest challenge of his life was in front of him. He was standing face to face, in the mirror of time, with the man he'd called father. Only Wild was the man who would have to answer for his father's discretions. Secretly his father was a traitor to the family, and worst of all, he was a traitor to the people that held him in such high honor. Despite these facts, Richard Wild was ready to stand and fight for his father's name. He was ready to die for the name, the family, and the father that he could never get himself to hate. This was Richard Wild's dilemma.

He stood with .44 in holster, his hand down on the gun and his fingers grasping the cold trigger, the newly polished pistol ready for battle. Richard tried to hold back his sweat, but water beads started to form around his forehead and kissed the ring around his hat. Richard holstered his father's gun. He was wondering how many people his father killed with this gun. He wondered how many people who did not deserve to die took a bullet from this barrel. Richard often used the gun as a tribute to the colonel. He never wanted to follow in his father's footsteps, and he never wanted to be a marshal. But Wild figured if he could put the gun to good use, it would justify all the bad it already owned.

That's what made this night so ironic. Wild was using the gun in the same manner his father did—to protect his name, making Richard more like his father than he had ever dreamed. Wild noticed the more he used the gun the heavier the trigger grew. It was symbolic as to how heavy his conscience felt. Something would have to give soon.

Richard still could not believe the situation he was in. For some reason, he was very uneasy on this cool, brisk evening. He turned his head and looked in a mirror that was behind the bar. He noticed a familiar glare he'd seen several times growing up. It was a glare that scared Richard, because he felt something bad was about to happen. He usually noticed it on his father's face, but today it was a look on Richard's. It was a look that was genetically handed down from his father. It was the look his father had right before he killed a man. The look would take another man on this day … it would take Richard Wild. Even if he was able to take down those who looked to tarnish his name, he questioned whether he was turning into his father. Was this the choice that would determine the right to move on as an honest man?

Was everything a lie? Was my father a hero, or had he been a villain all this time? He pondered.

Richard had three options. The first was to arrest the men he was about to face. Arrest the men who had already killed the young, attractive constable and quiet the town again. The second was to let them pull the trigger on him. Then it was no longer Richard's problem. The sins of his father would die with him. The third was to drop the men where they stood. It did not take long for Wild to choose the latter. He picked up the small glass vial that contained a shot of whiskey and quickly sent it down his throat before slamming the glass to the bar. He wiped his lips and unsnapped the holster that was at his side.

Richard quickly turned around and walked powerfully across the room and out the swinging door. He looked into the street and quickly walked to showdown position. Three other men stood at the other end of the street and slowly moved into position. Richard was caught off guard this day, as he did not expect the showdown for another week or two and did not have time to round up any help. His young friend the constable didn't have a chance; the men had gunned him down before he was able to raise the word *stop*! It was Wild alone against the three rebels whom had already killed in this town and vowed to take down Wild as well. These men were out for blood, and this day they would get it.

Richard walked to the middle of the street and looked at the men who were about to die. This was not America, and the old west had long since died off. But in Dover, England, this was still the way. The gun ruled the street, and whoever ruled the gun called the shots. Richard had no time left to think about how he'd gotten to this point. It was now all part of his history. Right now was the present, and he was facing the barrel of three wicked guns. Richard had lived a lifetime trying to protect his father, and now he found it ironic that the man in the middle of the line looked strangely a lot like his father and not the dirty man from the jail cell just two weeks earlier. This slowed and confused Wild for a split second ... and before he could recover, it was too late.

Boom ... a single solid shot rang out, striking Wild in the chest. The bullet pierced the body cavity and traveled all the way through the flesh, then came out the backside and continued off into the approaching darkness. Richard looked down at his chest and then back up at the man who had just killed him. He got a questioning look on his face as he dropped to his knees. As he fell, his father's gun spiraled around his dominant middle finger, causing Wild to notice that he had never put that finger on the trigger. In his heart and in his soul he knew he had never planned on taking a shot. This was his ultimate sacrifice for his father. He had to die so that the memory of his father could live. These men would no longer make it their mission to reclaim a debt. They got that today. Richard knew there were too many of them to try and fight. He knew that if he lived, he would be putting his own family at risk. He felt comforted that his wife and daughter would go to the cabin and be safe there. He was assured all the work he had done for this town would not be forgotten and that every man had his time. Today was Richard Wild's time.

As his body dropped to the ground, his head slammed to the earth, forcing his hat to roll off into the dust and slowly blow away. Wild's blood quickly escaped out of his chest, but Richard moved past the street and the dirt in which he laid. His thoughts were of his daughter and how she would live in the cabin and grow into a beautiful woman. He hoped that she would someday find a good man who could carry on a strong family name—a man who would be decent and a man who would take care of her. Wild had done everything anyone could have asked of him, and now his weight was about to be lifted.

The attrition of his soul was now over as he slipped off into eternity.

Eaton slipped his long silver weapon back into the holster, which was still steaming from the shot. He slowly walked several paces toward the debt that had just been paid. He smiled as he looked from side to side to see his fans cheering, but there were none. He wore black from his hat to his boots. His days in the rusty cell had done nothing to rust his shot. In fact, it did quite the opposite and helped him to focus it. His plan worked, and his emotions were everything he'd anticipated. He walked up to the man he had never called brother and looked down at the familiar blood flowing into the streets. This man was now dead. Eaton bent down on one knee and reached over the dead body to grab the gun he'd seen several times before. He slowly picked up the prized family keepsake and blew off the dust that had collected on it. He stuck the gun in his belt and leaned in toward the dead body.

"I'm sorry, brother, but something had to be done. Someone had to pay for what our father did to my mother and me. Someone else had the joy of killing him, and this was the closest I could get. Don't worry I'll take good care of this gun. Got many more people who I owe me a d'ept!"

Eaton stood back up a looked to his other two companions standing a few steps back.

"Let's get on … get out of this town before the real lawmen come." He turned his head back to Wild's dead body. "I got no more business here."

Part 4

THE CABIN

The fire was a nice one. Warm, almost hot, but too much heat was not possible on mountains like these, especially at this time of night. It was flat-out cold, no question about it. George had just finished his tasty dinner; the much sought-after rabbit flesh hit the spot after nearly two days of not eating. He leaned back in his chair and put his bare white feet back up closer to the fire. His toes were still a pinkish red, but he was lucky to find warm shelter before the frost set in. His socks and big army issue boots were sitting next to the warm fire thawing out, but he refused to lose his heavy winter army green jacket. He was still not warm enough to shed that. His backpack was on the table, and the film canisters and bulky film camera were safely out of harm sitting on top of a wood cabinet. This was home—at least the only home he knew at this point, and that was a comforting thought to George.

Next to George was a small twin bed with a feather mattress that may have been for a child at one time. George made it into a makeshift-resting place for his guest or his host—he still was not sure. Nearly every blanket in the cabin was covering the cold living body of the woman he had pulled out of the snow just a few hours earlier. He heated some of the water above the fire and then poured it onto her lips and around her arms and feet. Despite his better judgment, he took off all her cold, wet clothes and replaced them with dry ones he found in the loft. They seemed to be a perfect fit for the young woman. He heated more water and cleaned the cuts around her swollen ankle. He attempted to clean as much of the dirt off of her while simultaneously trying to warm her lifeless body with the water. Stone wrapped her in every blanket in the cabin except the one that lay across his legs, providing him warmth. He pulled the small bed close to the fire to warm her up.

She had not awoken, and George was unsure if she would, but he would enjoy the company if she did. He had some morphine and other small packs of medication in his bag, which was really more of a survival box than anything else. Thank goodness it was standard issue from the army base. George was doing all he could to wake this sleeping beauty, as he was hoping to get some food inside her stomach. He was not a doctor, far from it. But he knew what he knew, and he was hoping that would be enough to save her. He had been taught that food in the stomach was sometimes the best cure for pain. He made a small plate of the rabbit and left it close to the fire. He was hoping the sweet smell might wake her up. It did not.

It had been another really long day, and George was getting tired. He leaned back even further in the chair and kicked his feet up on a huge stack of wood that sat next to the fire. He took the blanket and pulled it up around his neck, savoring the warmth. George yawned a couple of times as he got a soft sense of satisfaction. He began to let his mind wander.

Had I not come along she would be dead! He thought. *Had I not gotten out of that plane, we'd both be dead. Why was I allowed to live? Was it to save her? Who is she? Does she speak English? How am I going to get home? How long will I be here? Now that we both are alive, will we stay alive?* These were the questions that George tossed around his head as he dozed off to slumber.

THE ATTIC

George,

I walk these streets every day. I pass, and then pass again. Later I pass more; I hope to see you. When I do I want to run to you, but I can't. The fence, the guards, they keep our love separated, and I'm not sure how long I can take this.

The days, the weeks! You grow inside me like a flower grows from the earth, sweet and limber, full of expectations. What will this world be when we are tight again? I ask, how long will this world keep us apart? Stay with me; I will stay with you.

I read out loud.

The notes were so personal. It was if these two people had known each other for a lifetime but could not seem to connect. The attic was getting a little darker as the sun was making its way across the room. The shadows were starting to change. Still, I was now set on reading all of these letters. They had me hanging on to every word, and I was not about to let them go anytime soon.

Eve, the notes I leave with the guard I hope you are able to retrieve. These writings are all that get me through the day. I rarely eat. I rarely sleep. All I think about are the days in the cabin and the days when just the two of us were together. The days when we were so quiet yet life seemed so full. I live in this huge camp surrounded by walls, but I feel so alone. The days on the mountain, the days in our quiet home are all that keep me going. I have to stop now. I have to get this letter out. I pray that you walk by today, and I pray you get these words from me.

This was like a movie playing out in my head. I decided to keep the words quiet and just let them talk in my mind.

I eagerly await you and hope to be able to see you as you walk by the fence. I know I cannot talk to you, but I will take to you in my mind, Eve. Wish I could talk to you if only for a few seconds.

Whatever this was it was real; the letters that my father kept hidden all these years were as real as the attic I was trying to clean. They were as real as the chair that I was sitting in and as real as the world that lay just outside this small space. But how could something this real be hidden for all these years? And how could something this special be forgotten in time? Where did this story belong? Where did it begin, and where did it end? Wow, so many questions that were never answered. Now the world has moved on. Time has moved on. The attrition of society no longer has a place for this story. This is where it lives. This is where it breathes. I have no choice but to read more; I need to know what happened to this love.

Your last letter brought back a lot of memories. All the memories are coming back. I hate this world we must live in. I guess I'm a little hard on myself. I blame myself for your being inside those walls. Had I not gotten hurt, you would have never tried to save me by leaving the safety of the mountain.

I have a lot of memories. It seems like anything that's really important I can't remember, but the smaller things I never forget. I'll never forget the cabin and will return often. I walk through the hills and see the paradise and I'm sure that you will be waiting inside. At what point do I open the door or should I turn and leave and never return. I hate this world we exist in.

Your face will never leave my mind; your touch will never leave my fingers or my hand. You have such a unique, beautiful look. I used to swear that you were so quiet when we first met and you never realized just how attractive you were. You were always such a nice person, and you always made me feel important and loved. I'll never forget that. Someday, maybe twenty years from now, I'm going to sit down a write a letter. Maybe someday others will know about our love the love that we will never know how to express. The words will be as if we spent a lifetime together. Sometimes we lack the energy or confidence to say what we want or need to say. I hope to do that someday soon.

Your eyes are the color of my soul.
But this no one will ever know.
Your face is the reason for my hope.
But this I will never get to show.
Your smile is the base of my fear.
But what I will have lost is real.

I wrote this poem today. It's too hard for me to look at, so I'll probably have to destroy it.

I love the poem. Please do not destroy it. I feel the same way: it's all we've got. The words are like daggers through my heart. Each letter I read is like a new drug to take. I can't get enough, yet I feel so bad when I hear the words echoing off my lips. I wonder if every letter is here. I wonder if something is missing. I can't wait to read the next one. I did touch you right? And I did get to be your friend for a period of time and you did write a poem ... that meant more than you will ever know.

I cried for ten minutes. It's a tragic thing when you look back and feel regret for something you could have done or should have done but didn't. I knew my time was limited ... I'm sorry. I think it's been locked up so long that the more I write the more that comes out.

While reading these personal letters I noticed that some of the words and some of the lines had been crossed out or torn off. Some of the paragraphs were shortened, and it was hard to tell where one left off and the other picked up. Strangely, the handwriting was very similar and seemed to jump from note to note. Was someone hiding something? Was there more to this story than even the letters would tell? I came to the conclusion that both my father and Eve must have been thinking a number of the same thoughts and that was why their letters were so alike. This had to be the reason. *No couple could have ever been this close or had this understanding of each other. Maybe it was the perfect match,* I thought. And if it was perfect, why did it not grow? *Is it because the world is not perfect and nothing in this world could be truly perfect?* I muttered inside my head. This read was becoming more difficult, yet I could not turn away.

The Cabin

The bright, golden light coming from the fire illuminated the back of George's head. The fire was so bright that his backside appeared to be a solid black figure or a shadow. It was ghostlike to Eve as her eyes slowly opened behind him. The color was slowly returning to her face, and the warmth of the fire along with the frostbite from the snow had turned her face a soft shade of pink. She was not scared, but she still wasn't sure what was happening.

The room is warm, she thought.

As she opened her eyes, she slowly panned them around the cabin. She made sure not to make any sudden moves, as this solid black figure who was in front of her would surely notice she was awake. Her brain suddenly collected a million thoughts, and most of them brought a great amount of fear.

What was the last thing that happened to me, and where was I? She questioned herself.

The throbbing pain from her ankle was slowly bringing back memories of the events that transpired. She recalled going out for firewood and getting her foot caught in the trap that was hidden under the snow. The pain at the time was unbearable, and the shock must have caused her to pass out. *But who is this person? Is it someone I know? It couldn't be. I live alone in this place of solitude.* Eve had crossed the channel and moved to France from England after her father was killed in a shootout in England. Her mother refused to flee and later suffered the same fate as Wild. Devastated by the loss of her husband, she decided to end her misery by shooting herself. These men came and destroyed their life and their town. It was as terrible as anyone could have wished on the worst soul, yet it happened to her. Now she was on her own living a safe and hidden life as she had promised her father. *But who is this figure in front of me? Who is this man? Is he one of the killers who have finally caught up to me, or is he one of the soldiers that now control this country?*

There were too many questions for a young woman who should probably be dead right about now but wasn't. Over the last few years so much had changed. A war had begun, creating much confusion for Eve. Yet it was this place, this cabin that was her existence now. But her little part of France was now occupied by the German army. It was their key port to the ocean, and it was one of the first French territories they had conquered. *Is this man sitting near the end of my bed an enemy soldier who found me collapsed in the snow?* She slowly panned the firelit room for signs of weapons or other soldiers. There was a rifle near the fireplace and strangely enough what appeared to be a film camera and some small film canisters sitting on the table. She continued to slowly search around the room until her eyes came across a heavy winter coat. The green army-looking coat was draped across the back of a chair was next to the table. It was a soldier's coat, but from what she could tell, it did not look the familiar gray German color she had seen several times. Eve strained her freshly opened eyes a little more, and with a flicker of light from the fire, she noticed an American flag on the sleeve of the coat.

"An American!" she screamed out.

This sudden burst caused George to jump and fall off the bed. He dropped the book he had been reading and fell to the floor. Eve quickly sat up and pulled the covers of the bed up to her chin. She had scared even herself with the sudden outburst, almost as much as she had scared George. The American soldier slowly stood up, making sure not to make any sudden movements. He stared at her the whole time and tried to put on a nervous yet confident smile.

"You are American?" she asked in her soft English accent.

"Yes," he assured her.

She looked the tall stranger up and down and with one hand began to pan her own body. Her clothes were warm and dry, and she quickly noticed these were not the clothes she was wearing when she left the cabin sometime earlier. Her clothes had been changed.

"You were stuck in a trap. I found you and brought you back here," George said softly. "Is this your home? Are there others that live here?" George asked.

Eve, still sitting on the bed and wrapped in several blankets, was not quite sure how to respond but quietly uttered, "My grandfather built this cabin."

George looked around and then turned to Eve. "Where is your grandfather? We've been here in the cabin for three days, and you are the only one I've seen. Does he need help? Is he injured in any way? Can I help him?"

Eve sat silent and confused, her long, dark hair crumpled aside her head. Eve still did not truly understand the situation but was starting to get her thoughts back.

"What's your name?" George asked.

"Oh ... he's dead," Eve suddenly murmured under her breath. George reacted with shock.

"I'm very sorry to hear that. What were you doing out near that trap?" he asked.

"I was looking for firewood," she murmured while looking around the room. It was her way of taking her eyes off him.

"Are you hungry? I've got some food in the pot over the fire," George called to her.

"Yes, I'm very hungry," Eve, replied.

George turned to the fire as Eve watched him closely. He picked up his rifle and moved it over to the side and leaned it up against a cabinet that was close to Eve. George looked at her and then turned back to the fireplace. He wanted her to understand that he was not there to hurt her, and if she wanted she could probably get to the rifle before him. With no words exchanged, both understood the offer, and both seemed to be calmer because of it. George picked up a small bowl and carried it to the pot that was over the fire. He picked up a small rag so he would not burn himself and opened the lid of the pot. He reached inside and pulled off several pieces of meat from the cooked rabbit and placed them in the bowl. He grabbed the rag and put the lid back on the black pot and then turned to Eve.

"I shot this a couple of days ago, but I've been saving some of the food for when you woke up," he said as he slowly approached her. George walked slowly and reached over to the table for another rag. He wrapped the cloth around the bottom of the bowl and handed it to her. She grabbed the bowl and pulled the meat out with her small, still pink fingers and quickly began to eat. The smell of the rabbit and the feeling of hunger from her belly were nearly unbearable. George walked over to the old stove next to the fireplace. He grabbed a small cup and dipped it in the cool water that he had been melting from the snow outside. He took the glass over to her and set it down. She reached out and grabbed it as he turned and walked back over to the table and then pulled out a chair and sat down.

"What time is it?" asked Eve.

George looked at his watch that was surprisingly still ticking after all he'd been through. "It's 8:47 at night ... France time," he joked.

"My name is Eve," she said softly while looking down and shoving as much food in her mouth as she could. "My name is Eve."

"That's a pretty name. My name is George," he replied. "Nice to meet you, Eve."

"What are you doing here?" she asked. "You are American. This is German territory. Is the war over? Have you Americans taken this land?"

"No. Things are a little more complicated than that." George looked down and got a little saddened from the news he was about to give. "It's kind of hard to explain. I was in plane, and it was shot down. Not far from here, actually. No one else made it out; I'm the only one." Both sat silent as Eve slowed her eating a bit and looked him in the eyes.

"I'm sorry to hear that," she offered apologetically.

"I lost some good friends on that plane, some really good friends. The only reason I'm alive is because I fell out of the plane. I landed about two days walk from here then headed up this mountain. I know this is dangerous land, and I have got to find a way out of here. I've got to find a way back to an American unit."

Eve continued to eat a little more slowly now. "That's not going to happen. There's nothing but Germans for hundreds of miles in just about every direction right now. This mountain is really the only safe place around. It's comical really. The only safe place is right in the middle of them," she joked with a small smile.

"What makes you say that?" he asked.

"I know … I've been here for years. The soldiers are dangerous, bad men. They would kill us if they knew we were here, or at least you. I'm not sure what they would do to me. I don't want to even imagine."

"What makes you think they won't come up the mountain?"

"It has no advantage to them to do so. This is a very wooded mountain. Maybe a couple of cabins every few dozen kilometers or so. And there are no roads. The Germans do not see a need to trek up this mountain, especially in this hard winter weather. If we don't give them a reason to come up, they won't. At least they haven't yet. That's a bridge I've never had to cross. They have everything they need in the town. I guess the only reason they would have to come up here is you. If they thought an American was up here there, would probably hunt you down."

"You're probably right," he acknowledged.

"They'd surely shoot me as well … aiding and abetting I suppose. Did anyone see you jump out of that plane? Were you followed or pursued?"

"I don't think so; it was night, and we were way off course. The Germans did go to the crash site. They were already there when I backtracked to it. But no one saw me. That's why I went up this mountain … looking for a place to hide. This seemed like the perfect place. Still, I found it. One day they might find it as well."

"I've been here for a long time. The only Germans I've seen were the ones in the town when I made trips down there. I think I heard your plane get shot the other night. I thought I could see a flare in the sky, but it was on the other side of the mountain. I wondered what it was." She continued to eat from the bowl.

"What are you doing here?" George questioned. "You are English. Where are you from? What are you doing in France?" George reached down and picked up the book he'd been reading but had dropped when she startled him.

"I came here over two years ago. It's a story I'd rather not share, nor do I care to talk about. Since that time, the Germans have invaded and taken over the town. I hate that." Eve finished her food and set the bowl back on the bed. She wiped her hands on the rag and then reached over, picked up the cup, and took a drink.

"Thank you for saving my life," she offered aloud.

"Thank you for living," George responded, elated.

"I'm not sure how I found my way to that trap. I thought I'd put them farther out. It must have been hidden in the snow. It certainly hurts, though. I guess I know how those poor little creatures feel. Still, you need to eat to survive, right? I thought I would have been able to get out of it, but I guess I wasn't. Luckily for me you came along, or dropped in, so to speak. Don't think I'd have made it out there if you hadn't." Eve smiled at George, knowing her original fear of him had already left her mind. She was beginning to feel comfortable with him and was even starting to like him, although it might have just been having a companion to talk to. It had been years since she had a meaningful conversation with anyone other than a French store clerk from the small town at the bottom of the mountain.

She noticed that George had picked up a book that he had been reading.

"Do you like that book?" she cut in.

"It's not bad," he declared with a smile and a tap on the cover with his fingers.

"It's one of the greatest love stories ever written. You should finish it," she suggested as George turned the book from side to side while looking at it.

"Seems kind long for me. I don't know if I've got that much time," he answered.

"All love stories should be finished," she added. "After a few weeks up here you will never want to leave," Eve assured him while looking radiant.

George smiled and walked over to her bed. He set the book down on the edge and then reached down to take the empty bowl from the side table and grab the cup from her hand. As he grabbed the small glass cup, their hands touched for the first time. Both stood still for a split second as something sparked inside the two, and it was not the popping or crackling from the fire. Both instantly knew something was there, and while it may have been the stress of the situation or the thankfulness of a life saved that caused it to spark, there was instant warmth to the touch, and they both felt it.

THE LETTERS

I *have no idea what to write—I'm a strong believer in staying close to the ones you care about. They are the foundation of what we are today. But the truth, it's just too hard to write and much harder to read.*

Yes, you're right … truth is hard to read, really hard. But this will not end in tragedy. You have to believe that this will not end in tragedy. It's all I have to go on; it's what gets me through the day. Please don't say these fences will keep us apart forever.

There's no tragedy. My finding you in the snow was the best thing that ever happened to me. Our short time together was more than most could ever hope to feel in a lifetime. People will try to pull us apart, and they may succeed someday. But you are in my heart. I will someday … somehow see you again. We will be together—if not in life, then in mind and soul. There is no length of time that can outlast my soul.

I don't have anything to say here really—just felt like being on this side for a while. I love your knowing the way I feel about you. I feel like stargazing tonight. Pick a star and know I will be looking at the same one. I'd love to hear your voice again. Write back one more time, k? Even a short note is okay. Even if it's just to ask my thoughts, 'cause they are all about you."

*Writing to you makes me feel so satisfied. I only wish I were sitting next to you and not writing this. It is easier to write this out. I'd probably stumble over my words and look foolish if I tried to say this. There is a reason for us, and that's what I'm willing to live with. I'm okay with that … I guess. I'm happy that you understand how I feel … tremendously happy about that. Knowing that you know—that you have been something so special to me—is a great relief. Even as I sit and write, I have a feeling **no one** has ever been able to stir up in me. Eve, that feeling will be with me forever; these fences will never be able to hold that back. No matter what happens, know this: nothing in my life and nothing in this war will ever—ever—change how I feel about you.*

It has been raining most of the day, so I went and listened to some frogs while letting the soft raindrops fall on my face. It was very peaceful, and the direction of my thoughts were very one sided. My feelings for you are very real. They were always very real … from that first touch that first night. From the time I opened my eyes to see you sitting at the end of my bed I've been dreaming about you. Every story you tell, every word you write I picture in my head, and it's like I'm in there with you.

    It was nice sitting out in the soft rain. I love the rain, especially at night when I sleep; during the day is another story. Soft rain on my face creates a great night—with great thoughts, of course, like tonight. In this dark place I wanted to let you see a light. I know you know nothing about where I live in America, so I wanted to take you on a mental trip of my hometown … a nice, slow midnight bicycle ride for just the two of us. I'm in the mood for writing. Would you like to come along? This is how we will spend our night together even though it seems we are so far apart.

    Here we go … close your eyes. Even though this war has torn us apart, you are still in my every thought. These words are for you only.

    As we leave my quiet farm home, we head straight out into the darkness and make a slow turn to the right. The street is really dark except for a single street lamp burning. We ride into town and make a left turn. As we cross over the first set of railroad tracks, we pass a huge oak tree. The base is nearly fifteen feet around, and it soon tunnels away from us. We begin to see just how small we really are. The dark monster becomes illuminated from time to time as lightning flashes behind it from a storm some thirty miles south. As we pass the tree, we smile and appreciate its size as a soft wind begins to pick up. We ride into the darkness again.

    We approach the next street lamp that is also lit by a single flame burning inside the glass. We make another left and head down the next street of darkness. The homes in this small town are older and as the wind picks up a little and we hear the trees begin to rustle, a soft glow from the many old front yard lanterns crosses our faces. We ride to the end of that block and cross over to the next one. A single white cat sits quietly under the next street lamp and stares at us as we cross, following us with his provocative eyes as we pass. Eve, you smile and continue to pedal down the rock gravel street. I can't help but stare over at you as your smile makes everything else on this short trip a thousand times more enjoyable.

    We approach the park that sits lonely off to the right. A wooden gazebo offers comfort from the wind that has grown much stronger. I suggest we stop and rest and talk. But you are enjoying the ride so much you want to press on. As we glide past the edge of the park we come upon the city swimming hole. It's really a muddy pond, but we love it. It's very dark as well. It's late September, so it's too cold to swim, but we can still fish there from time to time. I comment on how I would have liked to spend more time there this summer, but the months flew too quickly before I was sent off to the war. We ride off into the darkness again. Only the sound of the metal wheels churning, the soft wind blowing and the loud beating of my heart are heard.

As we approach the next street lamp we take another left and head back west. The wind now hits our backs and the pressure of the pedal eases up a bit as we are suddenly pushed by the wind. Off to the left is a white picket fence. The old man who lived there has been building it for years and it is finally about several scuffs away from completion. I remark how happy he will be to finally finish it. Off to the right we pedal by a huge old Catholic church. It's all brick and sits about five stories high and has a sharp, pointed steeple that appears to cut into the sky. We've gone by it hundreds of times but have never been inside. That will be another trip the two of us will share ... you in white, me in my best suit. The wind begins to skip around your head and pushes your hair around your shoulders.

*You smile again as we pass the small white brick schoolhouse. The building hides in the darkness except for a single golden lamp that sits above the entrance and illuminates the doorway. In the front appears to be a shadow of a dog—only it really **is** a dog, a big black one that stands silently in the night. I tell you not to be scared, because he is here every night as if to guard the schoolhouse and the children who learn there in the mornings. The shadow disappears during the day and then reappears every night. The silent soldier remains still as we pass on by the schoolhouse.*

We continue on to the next street lamp and turn left again. This is the darkest street yet. We ride off into a near pitch-black street. It's tough to see anything on the gravel street because it's so dark, so we stay near the middle of the road. Only a small peek of light shows itself at the far end of the block through the heavy trees. There is no wind right now. The block is so full of trees and houses the wind can't seem to find the path down it. A distant dog barks softly as we pass, but he cannot see us; he just hears the tires turning on the gravel and smells our human scent. You are a bit on edge, but I can tell it is because the road is so dark, and as we approach the final street lamp, you know the road is just about at an end as we cross over another set of bumpy railroad tracks. The bicycles cross the tracks as we are welcomed to the end of the street by a large old train engine that sits sleeping, waiting for the sun to rise so he may continue back down the tracks. We make one final turn to the right and head back to my home. The nightly ride is over ... only I do it twice.

The Cabin

"They must all think I'm dead!" George stated as he stood looking out into the deep black outside from the firelight inside the room. "By now, word of the crash must have gotten back to my family. They must think I'm dead. "

George turned to Eve with watery eyes. "The pain they must feel. The feeling they must be dealing with right now thinking their son, their brother, their friend is surely dead. And I would not be alive had someone not cut me from that plane."

George turned and walked over to Eve, who was sitting on the bed wrapped in three warm hand-woven blankets. She was doing much better now and had been walking for several days. The scar of the trap still wrapped heavy around her leg, as if it were still attached, but she refused to let the pain out. She was strong, and this was her way of getting stronger. She had made many leaps and bounds the last couple of weeks and would soon be back on her feet. Her new friend spent several hours looking after her, making her food, and cleaning her wound. He spent the mornings collecting wood for the fire and the afternoons hunting for food to cook on it.

For her this was beginning to feel a little like heaven. She had been on her own for so long. It was nice to have someone that she could finally trust— someone she had grown fond of and someone she was quickly becoming attracted to. She was not sure if the growing feelings inside her were the result of her recent solitude or if it was just having a man around. Just two weeks ago she could not sleep wondering who this strange visitor was. She even held a knife to his throat one night while he slept, questioning if she could kill him. He was too good to be true, and she was having a hard time adjusting to his dedication to her. Now, a half month later, she thanked God that she had not done something to ruin this budding friendship. This man was her friend, and he was on her side. He could be trusted, and he would always go out of his way to help her. This man was kind, and she was beginning to fall in love with him. *Is he falling for me?* She wondered but was not sure. All Eve really wanted to do now was find a way to help him because he had done so much for her.

"Sit over here by the fire," Eve offered to the young soldier while waving her arm to him and extending her hand to his. He quickly moved to her and latched onto her outstretched hand. Eve continued to add sympathy to an already overly sad conversation. "You are probably right. Your family probably does think you were killed in that plane, but think how happy they will be when they see you in person. Think of the smiles that will stretch across their faces when you step onto the porch and they welcome you home. Think of the stories you'll have to tell over tea ... or whatever it is you Yanks talk over."

George began to grin a bit as he sat down on the bed next to her. *This was a good spot for more than just the proximity to the fire.* Yes, this spot was warm, but his heart would be warm here even if there were no fire. Eve had placed a spell on him from the first time he set his eyes on her. He was not sure if it was the helpless abandonment that he was able to rescue or the beauty of her face as she lay in the cold snow in front of him that stole his heart. She was half alive and half dead, but he was able to nurse her back to nearly perfect health. From the moment he saw her, he knew he would do everything in his power to save her. He would not think about it until much later, but if had he not made it out of that plane and had he not landed where he did, she would have perished in the frigid temperatures. This was a terrifying thought.

Many nights George would lie in his makeshift bed, a few blankets in a corner of the cabin, and watch her sleep. Sure, he could have slept up top in the loft, but it was cold up there. While you could see for almost a mile out the top window, the scenery wasn't nearly as nice as it was on the first floor. Sometimes the fire would cast a soft red glow just as the embers were close to burning out. The glow would cast along the walls of the cabin and across the face of an angel. The red glow would flicker from time to time, and it was as if the angel was dancing while she lay asleep.

George had several fears in this temporary life situation. *First, would he soon be discovered in these enemy occupied hills? Second, would he be able to fight off those who would look to harm Eve?* But his third fear was actually his biggest. *He would someday have to leave here.* Soon would come a time when he would have to leave or would be forced to leave Eve. This scared him the most, and he was not sure why. In this world where he felt like he had to whisper when he talked or cover up his tracks in the snow as he returned to the cabin, George Stone's biggest fear was losing what he had just so innocently found in this little place of paradise. His life was in question from day to day. This was the way it was. But for some reason he was beginning to feel like his life belonged to Eve, and he could not imagine his life without her ... but he knew it would happen. How he would lose her was quickly becoming George Stone's biggest concern. It was now his duty to take care of her ... and love her. In a short time and in this lost place Eve had became more than just a friend.

"That would be something, wouldn't it? If I just came walking up to the door one day and said, 'Hi, I'm alive!'" George answered. They both smiled as they sat two feet apart but were more tuned in with their thoughts than they could have ever imagined.

"Do you have a girlfriend back in America?" Eve surprisingly asked. George, who was already still smiling from the last thought, got an even bigger smile.

"No. I used to, but she moved away … and I joined the army."

"That's probably a good thing, right? I mean with your family and friends not sure of your fate. It would be very difficult for me to deal with losing someone that I cared deeply about."

"What about you?" George asked. "You never told me what you are doing living in France, or how you got here."

Eve looked down and took a few seconds as she was quickly hit by a memory she was trying to subdue. She got a sad look on her face, and George quickly responded by reaching over and grabbing her hand.

"I'm sorry!" he quickly responded. "I don't want to hurt you. I did not mean to ask for an explanation. If it hurts you to talk about it, I understand. You don't need to tell me more than I already know." Eve, already holding her best friend's hand, grabbed a little tighter and squeezed tightly.

"I do owe you an explanation … as well as my life," she added. She smiled a bit and then took her left hand and placed it on top of his head. She rolled her fingers though his hair and then ran then down the side of his face. This was a tough story to tell. With one hand grasping his and her other exploring his face, Eve tried to find a way to get her story out.

"My father was killed," she softly spoke. "He was murdered just doing his job." George sat quietly but continued to squeeze her hand, adding support to a difficult conversation.

"He was a constable. Really, a lawman. What you Americans call a county sheriff. There was a man who was actually his half brother. They had the same father, but this man had been raised away from our family. He was a horrible man who robbed, killed, and did some really dreadful things. My grandfather was also a constable. He arrested his half son and jailed him. While in jail this evil man built a hatred for my father and his family. When my grandfather was killed, this man decided to pass on the debt to my father. This cabin," she looked up and pointed around, "was built by my grandfather's family. He was born here and would return from time to time as her grew older. He always took good care of this place. My father made me promise if something happened to him I would take my mum and come here where it would be safe. That was two years ago, and my mum didn't make it. I made the trip across the channel in a small boat from Dover and have been here ever since.

This is where I was supposed to be safe. Then the war came to France, and this became one of the most dangerous and destroyed areas in the world, right?" George nodded. "If you had not come along, I'd already be a goner, that's for sure. Well that's it. That's my story. No friends, no family, just me and the trees, right?"

There was a short silence as they looked into each other's eyes. The fire was still casting a soft glow as the darkness from the rest of the room collected. It was just two people from two different worlds brought to this one moment for some unknown reason.

"I'll be your friend and your family," George responded. He pulled his left arm up and put it around her back and pulled her close. His eyes closed as her head slid to his shoulder. She began to cry as his soft hand rubbed around her back. He refused to let go of the connection they had just made. Her tears slowly ran down her face, reflecting the flashes and sparks from the fire. The tears rolled down her cheek and disappeared into the soft green flannel shirt that covered his shoulder. She closed her eyes and used her nose to smell his body. She had not done that before. She had not been this close to the man since his arrival but did not want to leave his grasp anytime soon. She smelt America in the man and the scent of protection. She smelled the soft wool and male scent that draped his neck. She could smell the scent of logs from the fire that had soaked into his clothing, but most importantly to Eve, she could smell the future. The two slowly separated.

"Can I get you anything before you sleep?" George asked.

"No. I'm perfect," Eve assured him in her English accent and with a huge, adorable smile.

George slowly rose from the bed, and their hands slowly and eventually parted ways. He turned and crept for his blanket in the corner. The sound of the wood floor creaking and the pops of the burning wood were now all that was talking in this room. Eve slid back on her pillows as she watched the man bend over and collapse onto the makeshift bed he'd made on the floor. She felt a little bad that he had to sleep in such a hard place, but it was what it was. He looked up at her and smiled as a final piece of dessert to this meal of conversation they shared. Their eyes stayed glue to each other as if they were both hoping to send a message … but for now that message was goodnight. They each broke contact and turned over, hoping to fall asleep while knowing they would each sleep well tonight. The fire was beginning to fade in the rock fireplace, but both George and Eve were completely warm.

THE LETTERS

I want you as happy as possible. I know my place in your life. It's a better place than I could have dreamed, and while it seems like a disaster because of what we had on the mountain, it will never be a disaster. We had time, and time is something no one can ever take away ... no matter how short of time it really was.

I am craving this disaster! Out of every great disaster comes great triumph! I don't know why life threw all of this at us. I wish I were closer to you. I know there's nothing I could have done to help but still wish I could be there for you. I find myself wishing to be part of your life in ways that can never be. At least not now, at least not until this war is over.

I want to be a part of yours as well. That is why I call this a tragedy. From the cover of the book, our story, it's a good read and great story of friendship and heroism come out of it. But by the end you realize it's a tragedy that two who have such strong feelings are not allowed to explore them. I'm too emotional; it makes me cry sometimes. But hey, I am a positive person. Maybe when I am eighty and this war is over, I'll finally be able to look you in the eyes and hold you close for all eternity.

I understand your life. I really do ... 'cause it's now a part of mine. Remember this: it's tough to know what you want or how you are supposed to act until you have a chance to look back at it. Don't blame yourself; we are who we are. We are in the situations we are in, and we try to fix some of the things that we've done ... then maybe we can be satisfied with what life has thrown our way. If we are lucky we can catch it and hold on for the ride.

It's killing me knowing you are right there behind the fence. It breaks my heart to think that you are upset, depressed, and sad and there is nothing I can do. The other night I was thinking how we nearly lost each other. I'm terrified that I will lose contact with you.

I dreamed about you last night. I had a dream that you had been hurt some way. My dreams are very real even when you are not here. Are you still okay in there?

I'm fine, but I can't stop thinking about how we were brought together. It had to be fate. My life is like a long path you walk every day back and forth. Sure, there are some bumps, the cracks aren't always even, and some areas pop up higher in spots. But it's a dependable pathway that has lasted a number of years. In my life you are that one spot in the walk that is missing. Every day it's the one-dirt spot that when it rains, it turns to mud, and when I step in it, it leaves footprints the rest of the way. Reminders of the spot that needed repair, reminders of the part of my heart that needs repair. Now I'm like a gorilla in a cage with metal bars and a stack of bananas sitting just out of reach. Only I'm not sure if I put the bars there. Why would someone put something that my heart desires so much right in front of me and yet not let me touch it?

Why ... why ... why? I just can't take what could have been, but like I said earlier, there are footprints of you everywhere. You have meant so much to me in this short amount of time we have known each other. The existence that we live is so short, but the longing for you day after day continues to grow. Damn war—Goddamn bars, let me out of this fruitless, meaningless, lifeless prison. I did nothing but be born in another part of this crazy, mixed-up world. This place is driving me insane with every polluted breath I take inside these walls. This pencil, this wonderful tool of desire, is but a nub, and I have so much to write. What will happen when the lead is gone? What will happen when the only way to express my thoughts are to think them in my already over populated and crowded head? My hell, the hell atop my shoulders that I am trapped in, is the only place that I can find solitude and satisfaction. The feelings I once shared with you for those wonderful months are now locked into this skull, and I cannot do anything but relive them over and over and over. There is no future in here, there is no Eve, and it's killing me every meaningless moment I spend in this place.

Today if you are able, come to the lighted side of the yard next to the fence. Let's watch clouds ... see if you can find interesting shapes. It will be our private time, you behind the fence and me out in the trees. I know your sadness, and I feel it. I may be free walking around the outside of this camp, but I am just as trapped as you. Our cabin was not lived in for decades but it has never been so empty since you left. Our Stone Chapel sits and waits for your return. Our place of love is but a stack of wood logs and empty hopes. Let's stare at the clouds today; maybe we'll see the same ones and that will bring us a little closer.

If we never had those months on the mountain, does that mean I would have never loved her? **No.** Love is a special thing that has to be earned on one hand, and then on the other it's instant. That's love at first sight to me. I think a person can love many people. Falling in love is much different. I love you. I do not think I ever thought those same feelings would ever be matched. I don't know why your face is always in my mind, but I'm so glad it is. There was nothing there before. This love is different than any other I have ever experienced. You know this already, but I think it's important to realize there is a difference. More than anything, when **you** look at yourself in a stream or see your reflection in the vanity, I want you to know inside that in this short life there is another person out there who is thinking about you at that very moment. It's love, and that is what I feel for you. When my heart starts to hurt and I get sad, I think of you and that makes me happy again. A pure happiness. I've used the word "I" about a hundred times, but the word ought to be you. When I close my eyes and think, I don't think words ... I see pictures in my mind. It's hard to describe. You are the focus of many thoughts. That's what keeps me going through these hard days; you know how I feel about you, and you know that I love you. When I get out of this camp I will take you back to our Stone Chapel and marry you. We will live on that mountain ... this I promise. If the world will not allow this to happen, we must. Even if it's all in mind, I must know that the love I feel is shared.

You had me in tears. It had me in tears. Reading it ... and I had to absorb it first. I'm all rattled. For once I can't even come up with a response. I will meet you on that Stone Chapel, and I will be your wife.

I think I need to absorb it all. My heart is literally beating faster right now.

You and I connect; I think we understand each other, and that is a rare thing. Stone Chapel is our special place, and I will honor it always.

Can you feel this? What I feel in the pit of my stomach?

Yes, I can. You frequently walk me home—in my thoughts. I feel it too.

I love this! Tell me more.

You walked me home. You frequently walk me home. I imagine you are there with me as I walk back to the cabin. We talk about the cool breezes and how much colder they feel going up the hill than coming down. You point out how wonderful and beautiful the trees are this time of year, and I've always got some short, witty fact about them. We both laugh and then sometimes we sit and enjoy the life we are lucky to have together. You are always with me. You will always be with me.

There is a lot of dusting to do ... I need to do a ton of it myself. I am off to a good start! I hope you think of me as safe, 'cause that's where you'll always be—safe in my mind or in my arms. I've drawn a picture of you while behind these metal fences. It's my only vision of you up close. I see you in the distance outside and want to be there so much. I had to draw you just to look into your deep eyes. When I look at this picture, there are no words to describe it coming to mind. Some pictures are worth a thousand words. Others will take them all away. This picture is the latter. I love it. I don't think I could draw another."

Let's watch the sunset; it's always sunset somewhere. I think we have a connection that will last forever. I will go on about this later when I have more time to write.

I love your English voice. I wish I could hear it again. The cabin was so quiet, and your voice sounded so perfect in it. I want to fight my way out of here just to hear it again.

I love sunsets. I can really appreciate them in ways that many people cannot. It gives me time to think back on my day and realize how lucky I am to be alive. I connect with you in ways I will never with others—once again, showing a strong bond. I've been alone so long I forgotten what a great person and a great conversation can actually be like. We understand each other's writings, and that's important. What are sunsets like in America?

Kansas sunsets get pretty colorful, so what they lack in landscape they make up in large amounts of sky. In Kansas you can see the sky in full and the clouds and the sunsets. Here we don't get much sky. It's masked by the trees so not many sunrise/sunsets here. Miss those. I don't know how much time we have left. I've heard rumors of the camp closing and the soldiers moving on … and killing all the prisoners. Sorry to end this note on that, but I'd like you to know things in here are getting a little disturbing.

I don't think I could stand to see another man I care about killed. Please be careful in everything you do and if anything happens to you—know that I love you with every ounce of my being.

The Cabin

It was not long ago the hills were so cold that at night the small cabin would shake and the cold winter brisk night air would blow through the wood siding like it was a collection of trees in the woods. The air was so cold that George and Eve began sleeping in the same bed, under the same blankets, just to stay warm. It was easy for George to blame the cold weather for their relationship. The dual sleeping and cuddling to stay warm sparked a new fire, and it wasn't in the fireplace. George and Eve had fallen for each other, and it was more than the isolation that brought them together. The more time they spent in each other's arms, the more time they wished they had together. George had fallen in love with her smile, her gentle touch, and her soft English accent. He stared deep into her eyes and rubbed her small white feet. Everything he was doing now, this existence he lived, was for her. She was everything to him. George felt as though he could live in these French hills for the rest of his life. While he knew his dream would not last forever, he was just hoping that each day would last for another day.

These thoughts made his trip back to the cabin from the plane crash site an easier one for him. George spent the winter months wondering about the crash site and the fate of his friends, especially Dale. He knew he was dead, but he hoped to get back to the site and find something that he could have to remember his friend or to take back to Dale's family, should he make it back home. George was lucky. After searching the crash site for several hours and digging though what was left of the plane, he was able to find a small handyman woodcarving knife. George was not sure if this belonged to Dale, but it was very similar to the one he knew Messing had owned. Moreover, the knife was open when he found it. The rusty blade lay sticking out of the rubble as if it destined to be found by someone. The handle was black from the smoke and covered with dirt, making it hard to identify.

It was quite remarkable that George was able to find anything in the wreckage. Most remains from the crash were charred, and the winter weather had also taken a toll. The area was also well disturbed. The enemy soldiers who arrived at the site had taken any and all valuables that survived the crash. For some reason, they either missed the small knife or felt it had no value. But to George, this knife was priceless. Still, the enemy had recovered most anything else of value. He wondered *was this knife that cut me free from the plane?* He was a little disappointed that he could not find a dog tag or something that truly belonged to Dale. He would never forget his friend no matter how long he lived.

George grabbed one other interesting item from the crash: a small piece of metal wire that was no longer than his middle finger. It was nothing more than a small piece of wire to anyone else who would have looked at it. George was not sure what part of the plane it came from, but he had his own plans for it.

The winter months had passed, and the snow was melting. That made his walk a little more difficult due to all the mud now filling the rough woods. George had been a resident here for nearly five months and knew if he traveled he had to do it quickly, quietly, and out of sight. This usually meant long trips through rough woods, but George was okay with that. He always packed his sidearm and from time to time would take his rifle and collect dinner. But this too he would have to do discreetly. A single shot echoing through these hills at the wrong time might get him noticed by the wrong people.

George continued to walk and glanced at what appeared to be a fox in the distance walking the same direction as him. The fox was full of fluffy red hair, with a white beard and a huge fluffy tail. It seemed to mimic George's movements. Five months ago the fox might have startled him, but not now. George had been face to face with all sorts of mountain animals. He had seen mountain goats as white as the snow with horns six inches long. He had seen mountain lynx that looked just like the city cats he had seen, only a lot bigger. He had even seen what appeared to be an eagle from time to time. It made him think of home and the United States. All that would make him wonder about the war. *Am I doing my part? Should I be doing more to fight for my country?* Then he realized his effort was taking care of this young woman in this dangerous world. That was why he was brought to this place; it had to be!

As George continued to walk, he reached into his gray flannel shirt pocket and pulled out the small wire that he pulled from the wreckage. He took one end of the shiny metal and bent it over, matching the other end so both sides were equal. He then took his dirt-covered fingers and began twisting and spinning the metal until it popped and broke in the middle. He took the slightly large piece and wrapped it around his finger into a circle. The metal overflowed his finger, so he used the extra as a weave—in and out around the circle, making the small metal cylinder look like a homemade ring. He then dropped that back in his pocket and grabbed the second small piece of metal and did the same routing. Only this time, he wrapped it around his smallest finger. He again took the extra and made a weave pattern around the circle until it was complete. George had just made two wedding rings and was planning on asking Eve to marry him on their spot, Stone Chapel. The two spent the last couple of weeks collecting rocks and building a makeshift gazebo. It was where they spent a lot time outside talking, eating dinner, and gazing into each other's eyes. It was their place, where they shared ideas and watched their friendship grow. They were no longer friends. Now they were much more, and George wanted to prove his love to her by asking for her hand in marriage … at their Stone Chapel. Sure, it would not be official, but what in this crazy world they lived in really was? All they had was each other, and they wanted to make a commitment to one another.

George finished the second ring and dropped it into his pocket alongside the first as he made his way back to the cabin. As he approached, he heard some music playing from a distant music box. This told George that Eve was washing clothes. She completed this ritual several times each week. Now that the weather was warming, her job was becoming a little easier. To pass time, Eve would crank up the music box that sat in the cabin and play it while she worked. It was not very loud but gave her some well-deserved company while she worked.

George walked up to the back of the cabin and put one hand on the side of it. The warm sun had spent the day heating the outside wood of the cabin. It was a warm, relaxing feeling his hand was enjoying as he listened to the beautiful music and watched the wonderful show. He did not want Eve to see him so he could sneak a few moments of watching her work and sing. Eve was standing in the sun in front of a big bucket full of water with a washboard sticking out. She was reaching in the water grabbing clothes and rubbing them on the board. After several rubs and several verses of tune, she would step to her left and hang them on a line she had stretched between two trees. George had no idea what the song was, and he did not really care. The solo musical that he was able to witness was more beautiful than he ever dreamed a musical could be. Of course, his only other experience was with school plays at the playhouse in his hometown. He had never seen or heard anything like this. Eve had a wonderfully soft yet distinct English voice that seemed to roll along with the tune that was on the music box. George decided to record this moment in time. He slowly slipped around the corner and went inside the cabin. He walked over to the cabinet and grabbed his U.S. issue film camera that somehow was working again and loaded it with a film carton. George slowly walked back to the doorway and started recording, unknown to Eve.

Click … click … click … the camera made a constant quiet running motion, and after a few seconds it was enough for her to notice the soft noise. Eve turned around and jumped.

"Oh … how long have you been standing there?" she asked, beaming.

"Not nearly long enough," George replied under his breath.

"Stop that. Stop filming," she stated in a voice that made George think she really liked the sudden found attention. "You are wasting you film, and I'm not properly dressed to be recorded for some big American news agency." She turned back and continued to do her work as the music from the box inside the cabin lowered and then stopped.

"Would you crank it again?" Eve asked.

George turned his camera off and slowly set it down on the table inside the cabin. He walked over to the box and reached down, grabbing hold of the L-shaped handle. He started to spin the handle, cranking it several times until the music came back up to full speed and full volume. He smiled a bit and then turned and walked outside and up to Eve.

"I've got a really good idea," George offered. Eve just looked at George and smiled. She looked especially beautiful to George today because this was the day he was going to ask her to marry him.

She is beautiful, George thought. Her big green eyes really stood out in this sunlight. The weather had been so dreary and overcast George had never really noticed just how green her eyes were. Her hair was a dark brown, but the sun had started to lighten it in spots, and since she had it rolled up on top of her head, the highlights were really popping in the sun. Spring was making beauty shine in more places than just the green that was coming back to the leaves on the trees. Her lips were red and soft, and her cheeks were a cherry red due to a slight nip in the air. George reached up and grabbed her hand.

"Come with me," he said. Hand in hand, the two young lovers walked over to the Stone Chapel they had made together. It was round, and the walls were all stone. The two had collected the stones from the area and started stacking them until they made a design. The walls were more than waist high, and the floor inside was lined with the flattest rocks they could find. For Eve it was a chapel for worship or a place for quiet thought. For George it was the place where he and his love would unite. The two walked all the way inside and turned to each other.

"What are you doing?" Eve asked in her curious English tone.

George looked down and then reached into his flannel pocket and pulled out the two rings that he had made out of the shiny metal just a few minutes earlier.

"Eve, the walk back to the plane made me realize I do not want to live anywhere else. I think this is now my home. I think you are now my home." Eve stood in amazement, but the smile did not leave her face.

"You have meant so much to me—I can't even begin to know where to start. From the moment I saw you I knew you were the one. No one has ever made me feel so strong for something the way you do. I know I'm young, I know you're young, but I also know what love is. I know when I love something or someone and Eve … I love you."

Eve reached up and put one hand over her mouth and the other around the backside of George's head.

"I love you too," she softly offered back.

"I know this is not official and I know it's just the two of us up here … but I want to marry you. I made these rings," he opened up his fists, unveiling the two metal rings. "I made these for us. So no matter what happens from here on out, in our world we will always be together. I want us to always be together. Will you marry me? Will you marry me right here in our Stone Chapel?"

"Yes!" Eve quickly responded and pulled him near for a kiss. The two embraced for what seemed like an eternity and then George reach out and grabbed her left hand. He slowly pulled her hand up to his, gently rubbing her skin with his thumb along the way. He took the small ring and slid it onto her finger and then handed her the bigger one. Eve smiled and started to cry as she took the bigger ring and slid it onto his finger. The two stared into each other's eyes and softly kissed again as the music from the box played behind them. Above them the wind had began to blow and shake the trees a bit, causing a group of birds to fly out of the trees and circle around them before flying off.

"I love you, Eve, and I want to spend the rest of my life with you. I don't care how we do it. I don't care if we are living in this cabin for the next eighty years. Let's just find a way."

"You are such a good man. You saved my life, and I am not just talking about the hillside when I was stuck in that trap. I was dying inside before you came along and saved me. Knowing you love me has given me hope. I no longer feel the rage from my father's death. I no longer feel the emptiness and loneliness that had taken over my body the last two years. George, I don't know what will happen in this world, and I don't know where we will go but know this … trust in us. Trust that no matter where you are or where you go I will always love you. Trust in us, and we will never be apart."

"Who are you, and why am I the one to get this moment?" George asked.

"You are me, and I am you from this moment on" Eve replied.

They kissed again. Then pulled away and stared into each other's eyes. With each intimate breath both could feel the soft exhale of the other on their face. It was as if all the problems of the world and all the stress they had felt was leaving their bodies and dissolving into thin air. Eve continued to rub her hand through the back of George's longer hair while Stone lowered both of his arms until they were at peace on her side. He slid his hands around the back of her waist and inter-locked his fingers and pulled her body close to his. As one they stood in their gazebo staring into each other's eyes, sharing each other's hopes and fears. For this brief moment, their two souls were intertwined and felt as one.

"This moment will last forever," he said in a reassuring voice to Eve. "If this is it and if this one kiss is all I would ever get from you, it would be worth every second I've spent on this planet. You are my seashell, and I will keep you always as a souvenir long past the waves that brought you to the shore. Do you understand?" He paused. "You have been in my heart since I first put eyes on you, and that is where you will always be—even if someday we are separated."

Eve smiled then leaned close and gave George a second kiss.

"See ..." she added softly. "It wasn't the only one."

THE LETTERS

The last eight months have been an ascending fun ride at a state fair. When I opened the floodgates, that was the ride going over that first hill and heading down, you know years of building and not knowing where it might be headed and whether or not I would live? Well, the first time around the tracks has been so wonderful. It's a ride I never want to leave, even if there is a young kid sitting next to me screaming. By the time the ride stops, the kid and I will be laughing and walking out with our arms around each other. That's how I've felt the last eight months. What's the next eight months going to be like? In my heart standing in front of you my mind will be screaming and throwing my arms up, while outside I will be the man calmly sitting enjoying the ride. You will know what I am feeling at that very moment, and so will I. We'll be in a mental place that will belong to us. I will not give that away, nor will I let another enter it. We will share that space.

Maybe I'm the crazy kid next to you. I promise not to scream but to just quietly enjoy the ride. Also, I promise not to let go. It has been a ride, hasn't it? That was such a perfect analogy. Thanks for giving me a place in that. I guess there is nothing wrong with a little screaming every now and then, especially when you are on a fun ride! Since we cannot talk, let's go on another trip together in our minds … how about a nice place to eat? I know this little inn my family used to go to back in Dover. Stay with me on this one.

As we walked I noticed an old Hookah Lounge and asked if you wanted to come. You asked me what a hookah lounge was. I don't know … that's why we're going in, to find out, I tell you. It's a small place with Indian décor, and the hookah man quickly greets us at the front door. I laugh at that, 'cause it seems a little pretentious while you are looking around still trying to figure out what I just got you into. He asks us what flavors we want and then gives us a list of various flavors. I go with vanilla. Then he whisks us away to some floor pillows around a low table. Hope you don't mind sitting on the floor. You seem okay with it. The room is full of every imaginable type of English upper class … the young, old, different ethnicities … but the guy and gal are the exotic ones this time. Looking around, I am positive we are the only ones who do not fit in. The hookah man brings this giant brass jeweled lantern to us and tells us to inhale. "What?" you ask, and I crack up laughing because for once in your life you appear to be afraid of something. Try it, there's no unpleasant sensation like smoking. It's from fine

Egyptian tobacco. Well, when in Rome … it's not bad, not sure you like it though, do you? I don't smoke. We drink; talk, laugh, and I start to get hyper because of the very strong tea. You laugh at my antics and grab my jittery hand and tell me to calm down, and I obey your request. When you do that, every thought in my head, every motion in my body, every jittery impulse all fades away. This time you don't let go. I wonder if you are scared I will start acting up again if you let loose of that hand. "Better? Did I really calm you down?" you ask. Yeah, that's what I love about you, the calming effect. I laugh but then worry about what I just said. Did you catch it? You don't say anything back, and I start choosing my words more carefully because sometimes I almost slip like that. Thank you for the lovely bike ride last night. I went on that outing again this afternoon. I should ask you to choose the program more often.

That was a great time. I saw every bit of it. I'll put that one in my book as another must return destination in Dover. How do you pronounce that? Hookah? My knees are still hurting from the floor and that cushion, but it was worth it. If holding your hand takes your sad thoughts away, I would never let go. I did catch it, and while I didn't say anything at that point, I put it in a special place hoping someday it will have some company! I can't wait to take another; this one is on my dime. I'll have to put some thought into it, to make it special.

Just with your words you give me so much. Really, I treasure you. You are truly golden. Not sure if you know what that means, but you make me light up … even writing. Just reading your words makes me light up, even on my worst day. You may be growing inside me … and I hope you are. I hope to someday show you again what you mean to me. I someday hope to really take you to Dover. I hope this world will once again return to the world I was in love with so many years ago. How wonderful it would be if I could love the man I love in the world I love. Sometimes I think it's true that you and I will probably never have more than this and these fences will be here for the rest of our lives, but I'd fight to the death for what we have, and I would not change a thing.

I think you are right about the camp. They have cut back on our meals. Something is going on in here. You mean the world to me, and thinking of you helps get me through these sad and dreary days. If this is all it ever is, it is pretty darn wonderful.

Close your eyes and open your mind. I have just reached over and am holding your hand. It's more than just a touch as I hold your hand with my hand and then run the other hand across the top of yours. I slowly touch your soft hand and look you in the eyes. Are you calm yet? Do not think about what may happen in there; just know that I'm out here waiting, and I will always be waiting. Someday

I may be eighty and standing alone on top of a hill, but be assured I will be waiting for you.

Here's my dream. It's not one that came in my sleep; rather one I hope to share someday in the future. Do you like yellow?

We are driving down a long country road for no apparent reason and to no specific destination. "Where are we going?" you ask. "Just wait," I reply. You think to yourself, the flat Kansas lands are even flatter than I could have ever imagined. We get a small chuckle as I slow down and turn onto another dirt road. We continue down the road for about a half a mile when the cruiser slowly comes to a stop. You look at me and say, "Okay what's the big surprise?" "Over there," I reply and point just over your shoulder. You turn your head to the right and your eyes light up.

"Welcome to my home," I say as I open the door and walk around to your side of the auto. You continue to look in amazement as I open your door and you step out. I am home, you think to yourself as you glare out upon the golden field. You can't even begin to imagine all the yellow sunflowers that go on as far as the eye can see. These amazing long green-stemmed flowers topped with bright yellow petals surround a light orange hue center. Each flower looks like the sun shining on this bright and sunny day. The field is as yellow as anything you have ever seen, and the field seems to never end. Millions of flowers, you think to yourself. You turn your head to left, and then pan to the right. Yellow sunflowers line your vision for miles. It's like nothing you have ever seen.

In the distance … out in the middle of the flowers appears to be an oasis or maybe an old farmhouse that has been swallowed by the beautiful surroundings. They remind me of you and I smile while looking at the two forms of beauty in front of me. Why God made this world so wonderful and beautiful but yet so hidden I will never understand I think as I stare at you … and the field. There are no words to describe the view, only feelings, and that's how I feel for you, I say to myself as a tear fills my eye.

In a month, winter will be knocking at the door, and this field will die off and will be forgotten forever. I hope that never happens to my love for you. Why is something so beautiful and wonderful hidden back here on the back roads? Why can't this be out in the open for all to see and appreciate? But this is the place that it grows … and this is the place it will die … and that is what makes me cry. Maybe, just maybe, where the yellow touches the deep blue-sky … way in the distance … maybe there is another view. Maybe there is a justification for this field … for this love, I wonder. Maybe I should try to find another way into this field.

We walk back to the auto, and I reach into the backseat and pull out two handmade sandwiches. They, like many things between us, are very similar. Yours is turkey. Mine is the same. Turkey, no cheese, lettuce, tomatoes, peppers, and salt and pepper. We simultaneously take bites of the sandwiches. That's when I reach back into the auto and pull out a sketch I did of you just moments earlier. It's the picture that will forever be in my heart; the moment I knew the truth. I hand it to you and once you get past the fact that I am not an artist, you hold it close to your heart. I'm just glad you did not use it as a napkin to wipe off some of that turkey on your lip. Man, you Brits are kind of sloppy eaters. I reach up with my hand to wipe it off. You're not sure what I'm doing just yet, and you relax your head and close your eyes hoping that I'm about to do something else. I wipe it off and smile. Just touching your face was enough. We finish the meal and head home.

Do you think we will ever be able to live out this dream? Moments like this make me wonder about one word—tragedy. It would really be a tragedy if I never had another chance to touch you. I don't think I will ever work through my feelings, and they will be with me and beside me as long as I live. I know what lies in the sunflower field is nearly impossible, but I guess that's the tragic part. To love something so much and know it's out of reach.

True love never ends … it grows. What you wrote was so touching. I just don't have words to do it any justice. I will treasure that forever. I can only offer this reply to your dream.

When I turned around to thank you for showing me the sunflowers, did I see the tears? If I did, then I reached up and wiped them away. Maybe I even let my hand rest on your cheek for a moment after. My role in your life is to make you happy and be whatever you need me to be. These are the feelings you bring up in me. I see you in a totally different way than I have ever seen anyone! And that's why I know what this is. I'm so glad to be able to share it with you. This is a once-in-a-lifetime feeling, and you own the moment. Let me finish your dream before our time runs out.

*After looking at the most spectacular view I could imagine, I turn around as you hand me just the right sandwich—turkey, with cheese, lettuce, and tomato. I think, how does he know me so well? I **neatly** take a bite and see you looking at me, smiling, not saying a word. I know you just moved your hand, but I can't take my eyes away from yours to see what you are doing. Time freezes as your hand touches my cheek and a thousand thoughts run through my mind. I think, what's happening? Is he going to…? I am frozen, unable to pull away and unable to move forward. I leave that choice up to you and close my eyes. If you do what I think you might do, could I even stop it from happening in this place full of sunflowers? Would I want to? Your thumb brushes my cheek. Turkey, you say, and my eyes pop open. Oh, I think, stunned into wondering what I really wanted to happen. I have tasted your lips, and I was craving that more than the meal but yes, that* *was enough. And I notice that even though you are kind of laughing at me, you seem to maybe question that moment too. You want more as do I. I wonder if you know how much this trip means to me and that I would like to come back again someday. I also wonder if you realize how much you mean to me.*

I'm glad I understand you so well. There's no way in the world I could do it justice. I re-read it so many times. I'll think of you all evening as I walk by the camp and back to the church. George, be confident in us. I am yours as you want, and I mean that. What we had on the mountain is forever. We can't know how this will evolve, but I am yours forever, no matter what.

If only you could wipe away the tears that rip at my soul. I want to hold you. I've got to find a way out of these walls.

Please don't do anything in there that would take this away. Walk the comfortable path but walk along the lines, even the curvy ones. It will sort itself out over time, and we have lots of time. Someday this will be second nature and the questions will all be answered. We are inside each other.

You know how you can work on a jigsaw puzzle for hours and can't find that one last piece. Do they have jigsaw puzzles in England? I've found that piece and it fits perfectly. As far as what it adds to and brings to the big picture I cannot see. Once the piece is in place you forget where it was anyway. But sooner or later I will glue the whole thing together, put it in a frame and hang it on a wall. The question is whether anyone will know about that one little piece and how that one little piece is really the complete picture to me.

Part 5

THE CABIN

The day started out like most days for George Stone. He woke up as the sun cracked through the side window of the cabin loft. A ray slowly crept across the room until it landed on his face. He could feel the warmth, but that was never enough to wake him up completely. The morning sun would have to push on him a bit, at least until the ray reached his eyes. That was the trigger that would finally get the young man to open his eyes and welcome the day. But this day, even though it stared out like the previous two hundred and fifty days he had spent on the mountain, would be different. This day would change the rest of his life.

George leaned over and gave a soft kiss on the cheek to Eve, as she remained sleeping next to him. *Look at her*, he thought. *She's a goddess, so much so the sun never crossed to her side.* George swiveled around to the side of the bed and dropped his feet to the floor. He stuck his bare feet into his boots that were sitting at the edge of his bed then pulled himself to his feet. George stretched a bit and then reached around and scratched the back of his leg as his baggy gray long johns dripped off the bottom half of his body. He then stumbled off toward the ladder that went down to the living area. As he stepped onto the ladder and started his way down, he looked back to the woman who was still sleeping in the bed. He smiled and then completed his journey down.

At the bottom of the steps, a soft fire was still crackling in the fireplace as the shirtless American soldier walked over to a mirror near the fireplace. The mirror sat attached to the wall just above a table that held a white pitcher of water and a white bathing bowl. George leaned over and looked at himself in the mirror. He was a young man. His skin a soft tan although didn't spend much time outside. His hair, which was currently sticking straight up and flowing in about twenty different directions, was as dark as the night. George had not really had a really good haircut in several months. Eve had tried a couple of times with a knife to cut his flowing hair, but it was too painful of an endeavor for Stone to endure. So, he let his hair grow. His eyes were as blue as the ocean, well rested and healthy. George had a razor and had done a nice job of shaving the last few months. His facial hair was at a minimum, not that he could grow a full beard; after all, he was still a young man.

George reached over and picked up the pitcher of water and poured some into the bowl. The cool water rinsed around the bowl as he filled it about halfway. He took the pitcher and put it back onto the warm stove to heat the water a bit. He did this every day so Eve would be able to wash her beautiful English face in warm water. He was always putting her first. To his knowledge she never really noticed this small gesture, but it was just one of the many things he did for Eve to let her know that he loved her. He turned back to the mirror and gazed into it one more time. Something seemed a little different about today, but he was not quite able to figure out what it was. He threw his head into the cool water and let it soak for a few moments. Then he ripped it out quickly from the water letting the cool liquid spray on the floor around him. George had never worn his hair this long in his life, so he actually enjoyed moments like this one. He quickly dried and walked off in search of his jacket, socks, and rifle. His next job was to find food and firewood. This afternoon he would work a little more on Stone Chapel. These were his plans of the day, but they were plans that would never come to fruition.

LATER THAT DAY

George was never much of a hunter. He had spent several days hunting back home in Kansas with his family and friends, but he was never much for killing unless it was absolutely necessary. However, the past months had made him an expert at hunting for food. He could pick off a rabbit from a good distance or a deer if need be. Today he was. George shot a small cottontail and also dropped a plump pheasant and was looking forward to the dinner they would prepare tonight. George was quite the proud sight, carrying the furry creature in one hand and the feathered bird in the other; his rifle was strapped around his neck. George was dressed in his familiar regular U.S. Army issue green, but it camouflaged him nicely in the woods. His patient trigger hand usually meant early success. But on this day he had taken several shots to take the prey but had not made a kill. It was a good thing that he was able to get the rabbit, or he would have had to walk all the way back to the cabin for more ammunition, as he was down to just one round left in the rifle. It was important to George to never have an empty chamber because he never knew when he would need one bullet. Plus, it did not seem like a good strategy to try and get the rabbit with the dull bayonet that was attached to the end of his long gun. Animals tended to move faster than men, and while the shiny knife was good for stopping soldiers, it was not good for hunting.

George walked through the thick trees and back toward the cabin. It was turning to late afternoon, and he needed to get back before dark. Today George woke up in such a good mood that he chose a different hunting area, one that he had not been to before. For George it was a chance to see more of this territory he had come to love. He looked around as he walked through the deep brush and then came to a slow stop as he noticed a huge buck in the distance. It was standing all alone about one hundred yards away from him close to the deep green trees. George slid back quickly behind the brown bark of a tree so he could get a nice view of this large beast. The buck was three times the size of the young soldier, and while his bottom side was dark with mud, the huge animal was all white from his neck down to his tail. His head was tilted off center and looking back as if he had heard a sound but was waiting to see what would come of it.

George stood quietly. He knew the buck could not hear him there but would probably see him if he moved from behind the tree. The beast had a set of horns like Stone had never seen before. George counted fourteen points on the buck. *That is some kind of animal,* he thought in amazement to himself. *It would take more than the one round I have left to take him down, but what a food supply he would make the next few weeks, and what a nice blanket his coat would make for Eve.* But Stone was way too impressed with the buck to ever try and drop him. This was one of those animals that had lived up here in peace for years.

Funny, that's what George was also trying to do, live in peace in these mountains. *How could I kill something that so closely resembles my life,* he thought. He smiled and watched the buck as it suddenly turned and quickly darted off into the trees. *That is strange,* George wondered to himself, *not too many things out here will scare an animal like that.* He stepped back out from behind the tree and started walking away, the wood chips from dead tree branches cracking underneath his feet with every step. The summer months were approaching, and he would soon be ditching this heavier coat for a thinner one. Eve was good at that kind of stuff. She had a gift of making magnificent garments exactly to George's liking. He was looking forward to the summer nights sitting out at Stone Chapel in each other's arms and watching the stars. This would be a lot easier in the summer than during the cold winter, although in the winter he had the benefit of holding her close for warmth.

The sun had been shining all day, and this was truly one of those special days for George. He was starting to get thirsty and anticipated the cool, pure water from the lake on his lips. That was another trip he had begun to enjoy, the evening quarter-mile walk to the small lake and waterfall where he and Eve would fill their canteens and water buckets and then walk back up the hill. It was heavy work, but the cool clean spring water was well worth it. The lake often reminded George of a lake he and his friends would play at back in his hometown. Some long and hot summer days they would spend sun up till sundown at the lake swimming, talking, eating, and then swimming some more. *Dale was a really good swimmer,* George recalled as he continued to walk toward the cabin.

There was a strange scent in the air he noticed, but he could not place exactly what it was. It was somewhat familiar to him, but he had been on this hill so long that he'd forgotten most of the city smells. As he walked over the final hill and down a row of overflowing trees toward the cabin, he suddenly figured out what the smell was.

"Engine exhaust!" George sputtered out. He got a frantic look and a sick feeling as he began to picture a German army truck nearby. His first thoughts were for Eve's safety. He started to run frantically through the woods, but the thick brush slowed him down—and that was when he heard a voice yelling from the cabin.

"Halt!" Yelled a man from a distant call. It was coming from the cabin, and he knew it was not friendly. George picked up his speed a bit and came to a stop just in the trees outside of the cabin. He looked around and noticed an enemy army truck about three hundred yards down the hill near the road that was back in these hills. It was more of a path than a road. George had seen it a few times but never thought a truck could ever make its way up the path and to the cabin. He was wrong. He looked back at his current home and heard more yelling.

"Wir haben Schüsse wo ist Ihr Gewehr gehört? Wer machte das Feuern?" (We heard shots. Where is your rifle? Who was doing the firing?)

Eve did not say anything as two large soldiers stood in her living room and a third stood by the doorway rifle in hand. Eve did not understand what they were asking and refused to talk. She knew if she talked in English they would know that she was not French. While they were German, it was not uncommon to have a French woman living in these hills.

"Wer sind Sie? Was machen Sie hier? Von wo sind die Schüsse gekommen?" (Who are you? What are you doing here? Where did the shots come from?) The soldier continued to yell at her. The second soldier began walking around the cabin, knocking several of Eve's items to the ground. His long gray trench coat rubbed on nearly everything in its path as he walked over and pushed the water bowl off the table. It shattered.

"Oh!" Eve screamed out in shock.

"Wer sind Sie? Spricht mit uns jetzt?" (Who are you? Talk to us now!) The solider ordered. The second soldier walked over to the large cabinet next to the stove and noticed George's film camera and film containers. He slowly picked them up and began to inspect them. Eve, still in a bit of shock, tried to blurt out what little French she had learned over the past two years.

"Je n'ai rien, prendez tout ce que tu veux." (I have nothing, take what you want!) She tried to get out. Just then the second soldier turned over one of the film containers and saw the U.S. flag logo on the back.

"Amerikaner? Sind Sie amerikanisch? Wo haben Sie dies erhalten?" (American? Are you American? Where did you get this?" he screamed at her.

Eve could not understand him and began to back away from the two men crying. The second soldier quickly walked up to her and smacked her in the head with the film container as hard as he could. Eve screamed loudly as she fell to the ground in pain. She feared that George would soon be back and he would be killed.

George was standing in the trees not sure what to do. He had never killed anyone before and had never seen live action as a soldier. He did not know what to do. *Maybe they'll see it's just Eve and leave,* he thought. That's when he heard Eve scream in pain. George dropped the rabbit and pheasant simultaneously and swung his rifle around from the backside of his neck. He grabbed the gun firmly in hand and began walking hard and fast out of the trees. His anger had taken over him as the thought of Eve being attacked made him lose control. George knew he had just one shot left, so it had better count. He put one hand near the front of the rifle and the other on the trigger. He quickly made his way to the doorway just as the soldier guarding the door turned to him.

Pow … the rifle let out a monster blow as his last bullet fired at close range, struck the solider in the chest, and drove him back into the doorway. He fell to the ground drenched in blood and slid down the single small step in front of the door. Inside, the two other soldiers, still shocked from the loud gunshot, quickly reached for their rifles and ran toward the door. The second smaller man jumped through the doorway and right into the bayonet knife George had strapped to the end of his gun. George pushed hard on the rifle into the man's stomach to ensure his death and continued to press forward. The larger soldier, who was hidden behind the soldier stuck on George's rifle, pulled his rifle to his chest and began firing at the young American. Bullets quickly filled the man's back as George pressed on through the doorway; pushing both he and the quickly dying German soldier forward.

The larger soldier dropped his empty rifle and quickly went for his sidearm. George pushed the dead soldier away, dropped the rifle, and dove at the remaining enemy soldier. Luckily for George, he got to the soldier before the gun was aimed directly at him. He put one hand on the small handgun and pushed it back as one shot fired, grazing his leg. He dropped his right hand and threw a punch into the larger soldier's gut, which caused the man to stumble backward. George noticed the table was right behind his enemy, so he forced him backward toward it. The two men locked in an intense struggle for the gun. They hit the table with such force that the large soldier's helmet bounced off his head and dropped to the floor. George pushed harder to take advantage of the leverage that he had gotten because he was much smaller than the man he was fighting.

Locked against the table, George began to notice the man was slowly winning the war of strength over the gun. The man had also reached for his belt and was slowly pulling out a knife that George's knee was trying to hold down. George knew his time and his advantage were about to run out, and he was going to have to make a dramatic move. As the two men stood locked together, sweat beads poured down their face. George knew he had to make a move soon, so he did something that no fighter would have expected in this situation. He dropped his right knee and fell to the ground, while still holding the off balance German soldier. The enemy soldier spun over George, losing his balance, and then dropped to the ground behind Stone, swinging out of control. George twisted the man as he fell, forcing him over the edge of the table. He fell face first into the fire that was next to the stove.

"Ahhh," the soldier screamed as the fire began to engulf his head. From underneath the man, George grabbed the knife and slammed it into the back of the enemy's neck, killing him instantly.

"I'm sorry!" he said quietly as the man's sidearm fell to the floor. Still in a bit of shock from what just happened George stood up, his knees uneasy and about to buckle from the stress of the situation. He reached over and picked up the gun and stuck it in his belt. He shook his head, trying clear his mind as he grabbed the man's legs and pulled him out of the fire. He grabbed the red and white-checkered tablecloth that was on the floor, put out the fire, and covered the man's charred face. He did not want Eve to see this horrifying sight. Then he thought to himself, *where is Eve?* George stood up and looked around but didn't see her. He quickly walked back around the overturned table and saw Eve lying on the floor.

"Oh no!" he said in fright as he saw blood coming from her side. The lone shot fired from the sidearm had struck her and left a massive wound. He ran to her side and quickly knelt down to her.

"Eve ... are you okay?" he said while trying to find something to stop the blood.

"I think I'm shot!" Eve offered back in horror. George reached around the area and noticed a significant amount of blood was quickly flowing out of her young body. He began to tear up, as his worst fears were about to come true, but he also tried to stay strong as he looked at her.

"It's not too bad, but we need to get you to a doctor," he assured her but knew it was the worst injury he'd ever seen in his short lifetime.

"We can't go to town," she replied. "It's occupied. Just let me lie here. I'll be okay. It doesn't hurt."

George knew that Eve's time was short. He also realized there was little he could do to save the woman he loved. He did not know how to take out a bullet or fix a serious wound. If he did not get her to town, soon she would die. To him, it was an easy decision. He stood up, quickly ran to the ladder, and went to the bedroom. He grabbed two covers off the bed and jumped back down. He reached over to one of the dead soldiers and undid the belt that was wrapped around him and then tied one of the blankets hard around Eve's waist.

"Oww ..." she blurted out in pain. "Please, it will be okay. George, if you take me to town they will kill you I just know it. I don't think I could ever live with that." George grabbed her and picked her up. He wrapped the other blanket around her and carried her out the door, stepping over one of the soldiers he had just killed. George remembered the army truck at the bottom of the road and figured that would be the fastest way down the hill. He knew he could find a doctor in the small town. He knew his life would be in danger by taking this risk, but he did not care what would happen to him. His love for Eve overpowered his fear of being killed by the German army. George had lost his best friend several months earlier and was not about to lose the woman he had come to love. He quickly carried her down the three hundred yards, stomping through the brush to the truck, and then opened a door and set her gingerly into the passenger seat. He noticed the blood was beginning to seep out of the blanket he had tied to her. He knew the gravity of the situation but remained positive with Eve.

"It will be okay, you'll see. All we have to do is get down the hill and find a doctor. You'll be fine," he assured her. She smiled even though it was obvious she was in extreme pain. He jumped into the driver seat and pushed in on the clutch. He pushed the start button and the truck slowly and loudly cranked over; he put the shifter grinding into gear and let out off the clutch. The truck roared loudly and then began to roll down the hill onto a dirt road. The truck bounced and hopped as it rode quickly down the hill, gravity doing more work than the engine under the hood. The road was more of a small path than anything else, and the truck was rubbing on the tree branches as it made its way down the hill. George turned to Eve.

"Stay with me, okay?" George pleaded.

"Okay," she replied.

"What were the soldiers doing there? Did they do anything else to you?" George questioned with concern.

"No, they had just arrived shortly before you. I'm not sure how they found us or what they were doing there, but I think they must have been on the hill and heard you shooting for food." George looked away in disgust at himself that he was not more careful with his hunting. He'd been there so long and had become so comfortable with his routine that he was a little careless on this day. The truck hopped another hole and continued rolling on down the mountain. George had never been this far south on the hill and did not know what to expect. He'd spent some days overlooking the small town but never considered going into it. Now he did not have a choice.

"George?" Eve turned to him, holding her stomach. "I don't think I'm going to make it. Please stop. If I die, I want to die at the cabin. I don't want anything to happen to you."

"Don't talk like that. Everything will be okay, I promise. I will surrender to them as long as I can get you to a doctor. They won't shoot. They'll just put me in a camp. I can find a way to escape. Your health is my only concern right now." He reached his hand over to her and grabbed her bloody hand. "I love you more than anything. Do you understand that? I don't care what happens to me. We will always have Stone Chapel, and someday we will meet there again, I just know it. You have been shot, and if I can't get you some help, we will never get back to the cabin. If you die my life will have no meaning. You are mine, and I cannot lose you or I will lose all incentive to live. You are my life, and I am not ready to give up on us just yet."

"You are a wonderful man, George, and I love you … ah," Eve hesitated and then cringed with pain. "It hurts. It hurts really bad." George let go of her hand and moved his hand to her waist to add pressure to her wound to try and squelch the bleeding.

"If I don't make it, don't forget about me, okay?" Eve asked.

"What? Save your energy, don't talk like that," he ordered.

"George, I need to tell you something," Eve, said in a more serious tone while trying to look him in the eyes. "Thank you for saving me today. Thank you for saving me eight months ago. I was lost inside and out, and you gave me a reason to live again. You are inside me now; I just know it, and I want this to be special."

"Don't talk. Please just save the energy and stay alert," George begged.

"No. I need to tell you this!" George listened. "I was nearly dead inside when you came … and outside, in a rabbit trap!" Eve said, laughing and hurting at the same time. "You saved my life. Anyone could have stumbled on me that day, and I probably would not have cared. I think, in a way, I was waiting to die out there. I could have probably opened that trap with some work, but I'd given up. I think I'd given up on life. When you watched your father murdered and your mother die because of it, you wonder what kind of a world you live in. Is it a place that I really want to be? Then I come here, a wonderful, quiet place in the hills, and a war breaks out. More death and more confusion and misunderstanding—it just worried me. But the worst part, do you want to know the worst part?" George looked away from the dirt path and over to Eve. "The worst part is that in all this madness I was alone. There was no one who loved or cared for me. There was no one to make me want to live. I was stuck in this perfect little place all by myself. Then, you came along. I was ready to die, and I thought it was over, and then I woke up and there you were. This perfect American soldier who rescued me in this madness, and you weren't just this guy. You came to me, you cared for me, gave me the reason I was looking for to live. If I die today, I want you to know that you are the man of my dreams; I just did not know for sure until today."

George began to cry and then put his hand back on her leg and became desperately impatient to get her to town.

"Funny, as I lay there bleeding on the floor I was thinking how lucky I was to have you there. How I knew that you would come save us. I love you with all my heart." Eve began to cry.

"Hold on, I think we are getting close to town. Do you know where we might be able to find a doctor?" George asked.

"I've been here a couple of times. I think there is a doctor close to the edge of town. It seems I recall a wood posts saying something to that effect," she responded with confidence.

As the truck rolled to town, George could already see enemy soldiers standing and guarding the roads ahead of him. *I wish I'd have grabbed one of those uniforms from the soldiers at the cabin,* George thought. He pulled the truck slowly to the edge of the road and noticed another side road that went off to the right around the guard station.

"Where, where do you think this doctor is at?" he asked. Eve did not respond, and he turned to her. She had passed out.

"Eve, wake up, stay with me!!" George yelled as he used his hand to shake her leg. The blood from her waist had poured deep onto her dress and was now dripping into the truck floor from her leg. George felt panicked; he knew had to make a move soon. He examined the small town, looking for any signs of hope. Calais didn't have a whole lot left in town. Bombs had devastated this small village many months before, and now that it no longer belonged to France, repair was not the first order. This land was where many soldiers had already perished. Years of trench warfare had torn this small town apart. Those who chose to stay or those who were allowed to stay were the ones who would keep the town alive and keep the businesses running so the enemy could operate, eat, and survive.

George decided to take the small road off to the left. Fortunately, his truck did not raise any questions or suspicions to the enemy soldiers because it was one of their own trucks. Next to the road was a long wood post fence that had once been painted white. Now it was bitter, splintered, and gray, even broken in some parts. George was using the fence as a guide to lead him down the road. He had no idea where he was going. George saw a church with a huge steeple stretching up to the sky. As it was starting to get dark, he could see lights on inside. He turned the big truck to the left and drove quickly down a long, narrow road in between houses and destroyed homes.

The truck roared as he fed the engine more gas and bounced as the big tires hit the large potholes that lined the small dirt road. George got to the church and drove around the backside of it. He hit the brakes with both feet, slammed to a stop, and then yanked his door open. George ran around to the passenger side and pulled the door open. He grabbed his love under her knees and around her shoulder and pulled her blood stained body from the now-abandoned vehicle. He ran her around to the side of the church, searching frantically for a door. He soon discovered one and quickly turned and ran through it, carrying the woman who had now lost consciousness. He carried her into the church where two priests were kneeling and quietly praying to themselves. They were both dressed in all black robes that hung past their knees. One seemed very young, the other much older—although physically to George they looked the same. George rushed into the room.

"I need a doctor … I need a doctor. This woman has been shot!" George screamed out. The two priests stared at him, more surprised that an American soldier just ran into their church than the fact that he was carrying a bloody woman.

"Right now. I need a doctor. Do you understand?" George again screamed. Both priests hopped to their feet and quickly made their way over to George.

"Apportez-le ici, tirez-le ici par en bas!" (Bring her over here; lay her down here.) The first priest said while motioning to a table that was next to the altar. George didn't understand the words but knew the hand signals right away.

"Allez prendre le docteur, disez-lui que e'est moi et que j'ai besoin de lui tout de suite! Disez-lui qu'une femme a ete blessee," (Go get Doctor Peter. Tell him it's me and I need him right away. Tell him a woman has been shot) the first priest said to the second. The smaller man ran out of the room and out of the church as George carried Eve over to the table and laid her down. The first priest quickly walked off to another room as George put his hand on her head.

"Eve, wake up … come back to me, Eve!" he said loudly, but she did not respond. George leaned down and began to rub her head with his left hand. He could not stop the tears that began flowing while he was driving Eve to the church. He was openly shaking as he moved closer to her and balanced her on one knee. With one hand on her forehead and the other grasped to her left hand, he wrapped his fingers around the small ring he had made for her. George leaned close to Eve's ear and quietly whispered words that only she would hear. Hearing the words, her eyes opened and she turned and looked to George.

"Me too … forever," she softly responded to him. He grabbed her hand tight, brought it up to his face, and pushed it hard to his cheek. He had no more words for his love as he stared into her eyes. *Don't take her,* he begged in his mind. *Please not yet, I'll do anything,* he bargained with God. The first priest ran back in with a handful of white blankets and a pail of water that was still steaming from the top. He sat it down on the table and began to undo the blood-soaked belt that George had tied around Eve's waist. George quickly stood up.

"Can I help?" he offered. "What can I do?" Still in amazement that this man in front of him was speaking English, the priest turned to him and pointed to the blankets.

"Prendez les couvertes et nettoyez la blessure," (Take the blankets and clean the wound) said the priest. George was not sure what he said but somehow understood the priest's request as he reached for one of the blankets. The priest ripped the dress off around where the wound was, grabbed a blanket, and cleaned the wound. He dipped the blanket in the hot water and began wiping the blood away from the hole that was becoming more clear and exposed on her waist. George joined in and started cleaning, as Eve was still hurting and starting to sweat uncontrollably.

George quickly pulled his head up and looked at the front door of the church as it slowly pushed open. With his right hand he reached down and wrapped his fingers around the sidearm that was still stuck in his waist. George stood ready to defend his love again if needed. The priest turned his head and noticed that George was making a move for his handgun. He reached down and put his hand down over George's hand and the gun and then shook his head.

"Ceci est une église il n'y aura pas de violence!" (This is a church; there will be no violence!) He said. George kept a steady hand on the gun as he noticed it was the second smaller priest along with a man he believed was a doctor. The older man carried a small black bag and was wearing a white shirt with black suspenders and black pants. The man still had what appeared to be some kind of sauce around his lips. This made George wonder if he had just finished eating dinner or at least was interrupted from it. George felt a bit relieved as the two men approached the table. The doctor walked up and quickly surveyed the situation.

"Il faut extraire la balle maintenant, autrement il ne lui reste pas beaucoup de temps a vivre," (We need to remove the bullet now. She hasn't got much time if we don't.) He said.

George tried to stay close, but the doctor pushed him back as the priest continued to clean the wound. The doctor put his hand on Eve's forehead to feel her temperature and then reached into his bag and pulled out a needle. He flicked it several times to get the air out and then reached down and felt her arm. Eve motioned back a bit as the needle entered her vein. As the medicine flowed through her body, she slowly looked up at George, who was standing a few feet back.

"I'll be waiting for you," she said as her eyes rolled back into her head and her eyelids closed. "Never forget that I will be waiting for you."

The doctor reached back into his bag and pulled out a small knife and a small set of medical tongs. He made two cuts into her waist, grabbed the tongs, and went in after the bullet. Blood began to pour out of the two cuts as the doctor began to search inside her wounds. George was getting a little light-headed at the sight and stumbled backwards, falling to his knees. This day felt more intense than that fateful day his platoon was shot down. As the two continued to work on Eve, George got back on his feet and moved to sit down on a pew. He stuck his head between his legs and did all he could to stop his nausea. He began to heave several times, but nothing was coming out.

Unknown to George, outside the church several soldiers had gathered around the army truck that was still running. The doors were open, and blood was dripping from the seat. While a couple of the men searched around the car, one soldier decided to check inside the church. He drew his rifle in front of him and entered the sacred building, ready to shoot. He slowly stuck his head inside the building and cautiously moved around the corner. He continued on down the small hallway and into the church. He looked over and noticed the two men working and quickly moved in to see whom they were working on. He noticed it was a lovely young lady, and he began to worry about her welfare. He backed up to let the men continue working on the woman, but out of the corner of his eye he noticed George sitting in the pew face down. He drew his gun and walked over to him, immediately noticing that Stone was not a German soldier, rather an American. George was still looking down and did not notice the large soldier standing in front of him. George was wearing his army issue green pants and his gray shirt, and it was clear to this soldier that he was in fact American.

"Stehen Sie auf!" (Stand up!)" Ordered the soldier. George jumped in shock, as he did not initially notice the man standing in front of him. He reached down to his waist for the small gun but fumbled around in surprise and could not grab it. The soldier, realizing he was in a church, turned to the barrel of his rifle and used it to smack George Stone in the face, knocking him unconscious. George dropped to the ground like a rock. His horrible day of death and despair had just ended.

THE LETTERS

Let me take your mind off the camp for today. Let's go on another trip—to Portsmouth. Today it's only an hour ride up the shoreline. We'll take the ferry to Newport on the Isle of Wight.

We walk out onto the ferry, and I say, "Let's go to the top." You still don't trust me after the Hookah Lounge, but I say, "Come on!" We climb to the top of the boat. It's already moving, and the wind practically knocks us over. First, we watch Portsmouth slowly disappear as we walk to the front and watch for the huge Isle of Wight. We pass sea gulls, pelicans, and even fish are chasing after the ferry. "I like the wind," you say, and I laugh because your hair is so short that you would. The blue in your eyes really stands out in the sun. My hair is all over my face, and I keep brushing it back, but I need more hands. Give me a hand? You try to help hold it back, but believe me, it's no use. I like the fact that you tried.

We quickly arrive, so we run back and leap off the ferry. "There," I say and point to a weird little spot several feet in front of us. "There's nothing there," you say. "Just keep walking," I say. Behind the hill we slowly walk around, arm in arm. The waves look higher than usual, but that just adds to the English coastline ambiance. There is no one anywhere near, so we walk out onto the beach. The sand is literally littered with shells, so we lay our blankets back a little ways where the sand is soft. You brought another one of the American handmade sandwiches you love so much, and I get another chance to prove my eating habits but then I think maybe if I get just a little messy that hand may reach out again. You ask me if I wanted to take a walk. "Yes," I answer. So we kick off our boots and head out for a walk along the wavy shoreline. Our feet get wet and occasionally our shins, but you end up a little farther past the line and hold out your hand and the cool water splashes up. I take it, and we walk knee deep in salty water.

While we are walking I realize that this is not even close to the beautiful sunflower field that made me want to confess every feeling I held. But I hope you enjoy this moment just as much. Not even close to the sunflowers, I think, but this is my country, my land and I can see you love it just as much as I do.

Wow, that was nice. I felt every step of it! I only wish we would have more time on the ferry. Is the wind cool? I pictured it a bit chilly and the two of us standing arm in arm to capture body warmth. I would love to have more time on that ferry. The beach sounds beautiful, especially when you were raised in Kansas. My first trip to the coast was right before I left for war. The image you just put in my mind fits nicely for what I have never seen. This is every bit as beautiful as the sunflowers because you are there. We are going places in these letters that the real world could never match. Thank you for all that you have given me, and thank you for being you. I loved this trip, and I will try really hard to hear those words again someday. Tell you what, here's my version of that last trip.

Here we go.

I'm a little uneasy 'cause I've never done this before and the ocean scares me a bit. "Don't worry," you offer. "You won't fall into the sea." It's slow going with all the people. You smile as you always do, as a loud "Move it!" comes from the English chap behind us. I feel like knocking him in the nose, then I realize I've lost track of time a little bit because I've been staring at your beautiful smile and the way the sun has crossed over it. I jump and we quickly get walking again.

We both hop onto the ferry as I hurry around to open the door for you, but you've already pushed it open. I'm a little disappointed because I thought it might be my chance to hold your hand as you stepped onto the boat. You look around and then say, "Let's go to the top." "Yes," I reply, and we start heading for the metal ferry stairs. They are a really hard metal with a huge handrail that curves around in a circle as they travel upward to the top level. I follow you because it gives me more time to watch you without you knowing it. We get to the top ... only to realize there is another complete row of stairs to go. I'm okay with that, and I follow you once more. As our heads peek onto the top level and we approach the end of the metal stairs, the wind begins to pick up. By now the boat has started out of port and the wind has doubled in force. You turn and look to the back of the boat ... and stroll toward the railing. I, of course, follow.

"I love the view of the water as it flows by," I offer. "It's smooth and natural ... although I'm more of a lake guy than an ocean guy." "I love the ocean," you respond. "It never ends, and I like things that go on forever." As you say that, I instantly think of my love for you and how each moment I'm with you will be a memory that is in my mind. I'll be able to play it over and over in my head ... just like this moment.

You look stunning. The Portsmouth dock is growing smaller, but I don't even notice. I've long since left this boat and am lost at sea in your eyes. It's a place where I could be lost for years. I dream that somehow, someway, this boat is lost at sea and you and I are left to survive by ourselves on some secret island off the shores of Mexico. Just you and I together on this remote place that is as green as the darkest blade of grass and as sandy as any ocean beach in the world. This island is ours to share, just the two of us for the remainder of time. Suddenly you blink and the sun reflects into my eyes and I realize I was thinking all that in just a split second. How could this one person affect me so much, I wonder?

You start to shiver a bit as the wind picks up. It's September, and there is a chill in the air. I move closer to you to act as a wind block and try to warm you up

*a bit. Our bodies touch in several places and it feels really good ... really safe ...
meaningful ... fruitful. I search for something smart to say because at this point
your beauty and the bountiful ocean that passes by us overwhelm me. "I like the
wind," I say, as I fumble my words 'cause you hair is tossing around in it. You
move to keep it calm, and I offer to help, but what I'm really doing is hoping that
your hair will keep blowing.*

*You have a wonderful sense of elegance about you. Your eyes, your smile, your
hair, all seem perfect as you surprise me and run your hand inside my arm that
is leaning over the rail of the boat. You put your hand in mine and hold on tight.
We stand for several minutes with our hands intertwined as we look back to the
port that is now out of sight. I want to tell you how beautiful you look. I turn my
head down to yours at the very moment the wind is bothering you again, and you
shake your head toward me to get the wind out of your eyes. As we both move, the
wind seems to suddenly calm as our noses slightly touch.*

*My face is just inches from yours as we stare at each other. I love this woman
so much, I think, and I want to kiss her so much, but I'm not sure what you are
thinking, so I hold back. You take your nose and nudge mine a bit as if to say,
"It's okay, I give you permission." But my signals have been so crossed that I'm not
sure what to do. I run my nose along yours and then slowly pull back. That was
the hardest thing I've ever done in my life. You smile and suddenly grip my hand
tighter. I look you in the eyes then pull my left hand up and place it on your cheek.
I lean down and kiss you with a passion that's been in my mind and heart since
the first day I laid eyes on you. The kiss seems to last for hours as everything else
disappears. I close my eyes and picture that first time I saw you in the white snow.
I picture every moment that I've dreamed of you those days and weeks after. I see
you dancing, and I see you smiling, and all I want to do is stay in this moment
just a second longer. Then, "Ding ... Ding," a bell sounds to interrupt the kiss. As
we look up, we realize we have arrived. "Let's go," you say with a perfect smile.
"I've got something to show you." We head back the way we came, down the
circling stairs ... with me following behind, of course.*

*That's kind of how I pictured the ferry ride. Maybe a little differently than
you ... but that's okay. Works for me! Anything more you can add?*

*There was so much in that, it was so beautiful. If you ever find an island like
that, let's get lost. I swear I felt like it was actually happening. I love what this is
... I don't want it to go. I want you back, and I want you out of that prison so
we can enjoy those things for real. We've both had so many bittersweet moments in
our lives, so it's hard to trust this. It's hard to trust this war will ever end and you
and I will come out of it together. I hope the rest of our lives are an upward climb,
not as in a difficult journey, but more of a constant lifting.*

I was really into that last letter, and I hope Fritz cannot read English; he'd surely not understand these letters. It's hard to stop there, so here's more from the last trip ...

As we sit on the beach, I wonder and try to smile to hold in what my soul is screaming. I don't really have an appetite, but I take another bite to try and show some kind of cover. Did I make the right move earlier? Did I read the right message? Did I go too far? This love was so new, but it seemed so right. The moment was perfect, and it was a moment I'd been waiting for. Did I make the right move or make a mistake, I wonder as I turn to look at your smile. But to my surprise, you are already looking at me ... and smiling. Is it another message? The kiss on the ferry seemed to last forever, but now it seems like such a long time ago. I want another ... I must have another.

You lay back on the blanket on the beach, and I know you want to talk about the kiss. I'm just not sure I can take what you might say. I nervously ask, "What's wrong?" "Absolutely nothing," you respond. Your answer comforts me as I lay down on the blanket. I quickly decide to open up one arm and see if you want to be close ... you do. I'm in heaven. As I hold you close, I ask, "How are you feeling?" hoping to feel out the situation even more. The feelings are starting to overtake me, and I've got to make sure I make the right move. I love you so much. I just don't want this moment to end, even if that means sacrificing what I want most, and that's to feel you with my lips again. "Perfect," you reply.

Some sand from the beach has once again blown around your beautiful face and calls out to me to wipe it off. Would this be coy? I ask my inner self. No! It answers. So once again my hand makes its journey to your beautiful face. I open my hand and rub your cheek with my fingers, then use my thumb to wipe off the sand. "This face is perfect," I claim. Even though the sand is long gone, I continue to rub and touch your face. Your eyes look at me as if I was your first love, and I can see that. Your lips call to me, and I can feel your heartbeat through your skin. It's getting faster.

Then suddenly you do something that I never expect. You reach up and put your hand on my neck and pull me close. I lean down with a sense of urgency that I've never in my life felt before. My lips hit yours like the ocean waves slamming onto the beach. For every wave that crashes we turn our heads and steal another unforgettable moment in time. Your hand rubs and pulls on the back of my neck while my hand caresses your beautiful face. I pull away for just a moment to take a look at the woman I love. I just want to make sure it's her and this is not a dream. I run my thumb to her lips and softly wipe them. I did not make the wrong move. We were of the same mind, and our love was about to blossom like the sunflowers in the field just a few days earlier, bright, sunny, proud, and open for the world to see and appreciate. This was true love and for once we both felt it and for once ... we both knew it.

Okay, Eve, that's how I saw the rest of our trip to Portsmouth. I wish we could spend more time there, but I guess it's back to what we are.

George, you are amazing! Here's how I saw the trip.

When we sat down at the beach, the roaring waves were so loud we couldn't hear each other, but that was okay. I hung on to the sensation of the earlier kiss that still burned on my lips and in my heart. The loss of heat and strength from your body being so close was almost unbearable. I can hardly breathe. The beach was beautiful, but I was too distracted by a feeling of emptiness after feeling so much. When you pulled out the sandwiches, I wondered if you would fall for my trick again, for Pete's sake ... anything to feel your hand on my face again. You hand me a napkin this time, and it frustrates me. How can you know me so well, kiss me like that, and then just eat? Like nothing happened.

You are watching me and smiling, which makes me smile back, but with a frustrated sigh I fall back on the blanket. You laugh and scoot closer. "What's wrong?" you ask, and you are looking down with clear eyes like you know exactly what you want, and I think how I could never deny those eyes. "Absolutely nothing," I answer, smiling, realizing that's the truth as long as this amazing man is staring down at me. You lay down next to me, holding an arm open to invite me closer. And because I can't stop the momentum building between us, I accept the invitation and feel immediately like I just found home. You've relieved me from the loss of your body and strength but not the burning sensation on my lips and in my heart, no. That you renew.

Your turn—'cause you write the kisses really very well. I hope your pencil is not worn down.

I can't believe this wonderful trip has lasted three days of writing. Here's more.

I could stay on that blanket with you forever. If I had the power to stop time that would be the moment I would choose to stop it. That kiss, the way you looked at me, it's more than I ever expected. The sensations and emotions it stirs in me are beyond anything I've ever experienced. I'm scared that if I close my eyes, the reality will disappear. I can no longer read your words that I crave. I don't think I'll ever close them again so we can still be on the beach. The kisses go on forever just the way I like ... like the ocean. And again I wonder how you can know me so well. I'm surprised by the softness of your hair as my fingers play with the curls at your neck. The kissing is becoming more explorative, and you're holding me close flush against you.

How can I ever feel peace and satisfaction again? You make me want and need more ... something I can never have ... something I can maybe have. I'm just not sure which is which. I think you feel it too because you are kissing me like there was no other reality, and this could be forever. Could it? You pause for a moment and search my face. I wonder what you are thinking. I wish I could tell you not to think, just do, because it would be easy here. I wonder if you have any idea the effect your touch has on me. Do you know how you make me happy? How you make me a better person if only through seeing myself through your eyes?

After wiping sand from my face, you make a decision, and it's one I like. You kiss me again and without losing our connection, your hands pull you up over on top of me. The feeling of our whole bodies touching sends a shiver down my spine. My mind is on overload wondering what you will do next. I want you to tell me everything—how you feel, what you want, but the moment is suddenly washed away. We did not notice the tide come in. Warm Isle of Wight water rolls through us. We laugh at the distraction but are relieved at the chill the wind created against our wet clothes. I realize that I lose my ability to think straight around you, and I'm okay with that. This love will go at it's own pace.

Once again my life revolves around your letters. Even out here, this place I live is nothing compared to the world you and I have created on paper. That's our theme ... something always happens to bring us back to reality. A ferry bell or a wave crashing down to break what is not real and remind us of what we can strive for ... and it's okay. We'll come back here or go somewhere else and keep trying until that old pesky reality leaves us alone and brings us something new.

Don't know if my body or mind could take more. That was as good as it gets. I pictured me pulling us over and you rolling on top and I began to melt! Oh my. You are such a great writer, and it seems like we are always on the same page. You can write a situation, and I can take it from there, and you can pick it right up. I hope we get a chance to sit in the cabin and write together, then live it for real. My face is always burning, my heart is always racing, and my soul is so alive these days because of all these perfect moments you give me. You are the perfect gift. I don't even know why it was given to me, but I will always cherish it. Then I hope and pray that I will have it for the remainder of my days.

The moment is perfect. I don't know what comes over me when I sit down to write, but just thinking of you takes me to places that I love and want to experience. You are so good to me, and we have come so far in such a short time. Just think of how far we still have to go. I am a gift for you for some reason. Somehow I am here for you. You are a gift to me as well. You have taken in all my feelings and have watched them grow. I will never be able to thank you enough for that. I did not know it was possible to love you more than I already did ... now I know that it is.

I am a long way from perfect, but when I'm with you ... I want to be. I will always be open and honest with you about everything. That is a promise. That's why it's so hard for me to tell you what is going on in here. Some other prisoners have been taken away and have never returned. I think some have been killed, and I fear that being the only American in here, my day might be coming soon.

I can't take this, and I can't take what is happening to you. Sometimes I want to steal a truck and crash it through the gates to get you out. I just try to sit and wait and maybe something good will come of all of this. That's what happened on the mountain. I was waiting and you came for me. It's true that I would love to be so much more, but I understand where that is at, and I will wait. And while it hurts a bit, I've learned to live without you for a long time ... so I can wait longer if I have to. Just please try to find a way to stay alive in there. We have a world worth fighting for out here. If something happens and you have to break contact with me, that would hurt tremendously, but I will do whatever you need. If getting me these letters is too risky, just tell me what you need to be safe.

Where would my life be right now if you had never entered it? I would be just a little sadder and maybe not know why. Do you think there is ever a way to stay in a moment and not think about everything else, maybe a chance to be at one outside all of this and then return to sanity? This I'm not sure. I've missed you so much over time that it's hard to compare anything to this pain. It's like when you've cared for someone so long—other time is meaningless and wasteful. I will wait to see you, but I cannot wait. Does that make sense? It was just so natural and felt so right I don't even know when it first happened. I just knew I could not stop watching you. Not one part of my brain or body argued about it. Just that it meant the world to me, and I knew that whatever we were doing and how we ended up together was somehow right. George, you write beautifully and are always touching my heart. The world would be a nicer place if everyone experienced life the way you do ... and I.

I don't know why this is happening I just know it's ours and it makes me happy. I hope it makes you happy too. I don't ever want this to cause you worry. Falling down for me would be making you sad. It would mean losing this and losing what we had at Stone Chapel, and I don't ever want to lose that. Tomorrow let's find a way to meet at the fence and touch. I will be near the southeast corner on the church side. Please find me.

I hope to feel that feeling in my body ... the one I could not control today at the fence. The shaking, the touch, and the feeling of a soft hand from you rubbing my hand and my arm were almost too much. The blissful feeling and the brief connection that we made helped me forget the bleakness of my imprisonment. I hope to feel that again … and again … and again. That is true love. It is rare, but I hope to feel it again. That is all that I hope for. I only hope that you don't think less of me now. I'm dirty, stinky, and appear to be a mess at least on the outside, but you are keeping me sane on the inside. Thank you for the few seconds we were able to have. I fear that may have been the last time we ever touch, but I desperately hope there will be many more. Please hold on tight to my hand just like you did moments ago.

Okay—I'll hold tight. If you fall, I will fall with you.

Maybe my mind can see things my brain will not accept. And that is why I dream about them. That is where I have no control. When I realize it's just a dream and I can change the outcome, I wake up before I can do anything about it. That's what is going on here. I have no control, and I can't do anything about it. If these soldiers do not kill me, surely the waiting will.

I don't know if we've climaxed yet. I feel so empty without you. I refuse to believe it's all downhill from here; that thought makes me very sad. The only thing that can come between us is us, right? You do what you have to do to stay alive, and I'll be right here waiting for you. I will always be waiting for you on that mountain. Not only do I feel very loved, but I also feel like I've always been cared for, and it's changed my perspective on my past and what happened with my father. You've rewritten my history. I regret any moment I have not been there for you. I hope our future is always together in any form, life, or world.

THE CAMP

It was the metal fence that stood between George and the life he had fallen in love with. Now that time on the mountain in his Stone Chapel seemed like years ago. The air was turning cold, and snow had started to fall. Despite the dreary weather, Stone refused to wear a winter coat. The soldier guarding the camp had issued him one, as well as a bunk and a cover in a room with fifty other prisoners. The coat spent most of the day lying on his bed, his new home in this world. It was a world of barbed wire and high fences, guard towers, and soldiers with guns. There was an alarm and roll call every morning at 6:00 a.m. and a lights-out call at 8:00 p.m. There were two meals a day, although George rarely felt like eating. The camp food was nothing more than mush; George did not know what was in it and did not care. That's why he rarely ate. His day now consisted of writing letters.

George Stone was very lucky because the guard who arrested him several months earlier in the church could have been a friend had they not been on opposite sides in a war. The soldier, Fritz, was a large man. He was in his mid-forties, had brown hair that was graying and a big belly, and he did not want to be in this war. His English was broken at best, or at least as good as George's German. Yet they had connected on one very similar topic: when Fritz arrested George in the church, he quickly understood what Stone was doing.

Fritz understood Stone was risking his own life to save the young French woman who was bleeding in the church, and this played to the large German soldier's softer side. Fritz had honor and respect for George and wished they could have been friends. He was in the war for the same reason as George, not to kill but to fight for what his country believed was right. His wife was shot and killed during the war a couple of years earlier, but no one knew how or when. They found her lying in the grass at his home just across the border, and no one was there to help her. Although Fritz was hurt inside, he wasn't emotionally dead—in fact, just the opposite. This was why he admired George so much and went out of his way to look after him in the camp. Plus, Stone was the only American prisoner is this camp, and that made him a bit of a celebrity to the German soldiers.

George was not really aware of all Fritz had done for him to keep him healthy and alive but probably would not have cared much anyway, as he was still a prisoner. But there was one thing that Fritz would do for George nearly every day that Stone would never forget. About a month after George was arrested and the church took in Eve, George noticed her walking outside the fence. George tried to talk to her, but the guards would never let him get that close to her. Fritz could not allow George to get close to the fence but offered to exchange letters between the two young lovers. George spent most of his days writing, and Fritz would take the letter outside the gate at the end of his shift and give it to Eve. She would then write back at night, give the letter to Fritz, and he would take it to George in the morning. Sometimes he was able to make the switch two or three times a day for Stone. This was all Fritz could do to help George communicate with Eve. From time to time he would sit and talk to George, trying to figure out what the two were talking about, although there was always a language barrier. This was also very risky for Fritz. If he was discovered aiding the enemy, he could face harsh punishment from the Germans. Still, he did what he could because he felt a little guilty for separating the two lovers.

While the days in the camp were long and boring to George, he looked forward to his morning mail more than anything. Sadly, Fritz demanded that any letter Eve would send into the camp for George to read would have to go back out of camp with his letter that night. That was to ensure that no one would find the secret letters and Fritz would not get in trouble. This meant George would have to let the letters live in his mind. He would read each one hundreds of times before writing his response back so he could memorize almost every line. It's what got him through the long, dreary, lonely, painful days.

Eve had been taken in by the church and cared for from the time George took her there. The two priests helped nurse her wounds and helped her get back on her feet and healthy again. Eve did have some complications, and so the French priests demanded that she live with them. Although she had been wounded, she had grown into her age and had put on some weight, Eve had not returned to the cabin since the attack. She did not have the stamina nor the desire to return there without George. Eve Wild was lucky to be alive, although she would have gladly given her life so George would not be trapped like an animal in a cage. Still, they were able to communicate, and this got her through the day. It was also the reason she had not made the trip back up the hill; she didn't want to leave George alone in the camp.

Her daily walks by the camp meant the world to both of them. Their eyes would meet and stay connected from the corner of the gate until she walked out of sight near the church. Over the last few months the two had arranged a schedule of when they would see each other, but their true desire was to hear the sound and the tone of the other's voice. Eve was doing odd jobs around the church, cleaning, walking to the store, and doing other jobs that would keep her at the church. Still, it was her way of thanking the priests who helped save her life. She did all she could to help them. But most of her time was spent writing her thoughts back to George. It wasn't perfect, but it was all that mattered to Eve.

George was a little less impatient. With each letter he wrote he grew a little more weary and tired of the camp. He had not shaved in months and had grown a beard. He was only allowed to shower once every few weeks, so most of the time he had a foul odor. His hair had grown past his ears, and now it was past his neck. His hands were dirty; his nails close to black, and only when he bit them off were they ever cleaned. He had worn the same shirt for the last few months, and it had begun to frazzle and tear around the sleeves. Bloodstains from Eve still lined his shirt. It seemed the dirt and dust of this place was embedded in his mind as well as his clothes.

While Eve had gained weight, George had lost several pounds over the last few months. He knew that in order to stay alive and see Eve again, he would need to start wearing the heavy winter coat. Deep in his heart, he knew that eventually he would find a way to be with Eve again. George was never much of a poet or a writer as a child but had improved over the last several months. Eve brought that out in him. He titled his writings, poems, and letters his attrition—although he never got to keep them. Eve had collected all of the notes and letters and kept close watch over them with her personal items at the church. These words were his wearing of the soul, and he had to find a way to beat them. All he had to do was get out of this hole and run off with Eve, yet an army held him back.

This was not the war George signed up for; he was supposed to see the world with Dale. His friend was the writer, and George's job was to capture the film so people all over the world would know what was going on in this war. That was how he wanted to help his country, and that was what he thought would make his family proud. He did not expect to be the only survivor on his first mission. He did not expect to lose his best friend. He did not expect that his family would fear he was dead and he might soon be forgotten. But what he really did not expect was to fall in love, and he certainly did not expect to be trapped in this place without a chance to explore that love.

At times his thinking began to drive him mad, and that's why he started writing. It was his ability to communicate with Eve that kept him sane. Still, from time to time he would get really sad and write poems that would mentally bring him down.

LETTER TO MY HEART

Heart, why do you hurt?

Love is positive, love is good, so why all the pain?

I don't understand ... why can't these feelings I have make you feel satisfied?

They are such wonderful feelings.

The rest of my body, mind, and soul feel so good when I deal with this issue ... why can't you?

I was born to love this person and every piece of my soul tells me that's what I'm supposed to do, so why the pain with you?

Why can't you feel the same glow that the eyes feel when I see her?

Or feel the same euphoria my mind feels when I think of her, the same sweet hum my ears feel when I hear her voice, or the everlasting ecstasy my hands feel when I touch her?

Every part of my body longs to fulfill this feeling but you stand out.

Your ache overrides almost everything else that tempts my senses.

You are dominant ... why?

Why can you let this be?

Will you ache forever ... because I will love forever?

Part 6

THE LETTERS

I'll wait until I'm eighty if I have to. I'll reread a letter to your heart and cry because it's exactly how I feel. It's the only time my heart will truly rest, when I see you or hear your voice. I'm glad you are safe, and I hope the weather clears for you. I sometimes like the rain. I can change your perspective on rain. Here is another mental trip, okay?

We are stuck under our Stone Chapel gazebo and it starts to drizzle. I know it's late and we should be going inside. It was such a wonderful evening under the gazebo that we are both putting off heading to bed because we want to spend more time together in this wonderful place. The days are too short. I go to bed but can't wait to wake up in your arms the next day. The wind is picking up, and you and I are so wrapped up in each other that we don't notice it starts to rain. The rain becomes heavy, and the wind blows it in our direction. It finally catches our attention, and we realize just how late it is. We talk about how we should be getting inside, and I think of how many hours I would stand out in the cool drops just to be with you. I've already lost my heart to you. I already crave your touch. The wind is dying, but the rain becomes even heavier, like a sheet surrounding the gazebo. We look at each other and smile. We're stuck.

As I look at your soft hair blowing gently in the wind, my first reaction is to wipe it from your eyes—but I can't. I love your hair blowing in the wind, so I react up and rub your cheek. It might be the only part of your body and soul that I can't see right now thanks to the blowing hair. I brush the strands away from your ear so I can see it and complete your beautiful face. I have now seen all of you on this night ... mentally and physically—at least as much as time will allow. I think, oh, no time! But my love for you has nothing but time to give.

I look down to my watch. Unfortunately, it's still ticking. But lucky for me I always wear it very loose so the face of the watch gives way to gravity and pulls to the ground. That way if I want to know what time it is I will physically have to work to find out. I don't want to know, so I look back up to your eyes. I pull you close to ensure safety on this quiet night as the mist of dew begins to fall. I hold you close and take one hand and rub it along your back. How many times have I dreamed of touching this back? Well, it matters little; at this **moment** *you belong to me: body and mind. This touch is surely mine … and the look of love in your eyes belongs to me as well, and I will keep it forever. I once called you my sky at sunset, always beautiful and always out of reach, but on this dark night, shadowed only by the outline of a stone gazebo, the sunset is in the palm of my hand. Can I keep it there? No, it will soon return to the stars. The rain reminds me of this! The soft drops are now as loud as ball bearings hitting a tin roof. They've become a million alarm clocks that are roaring it's time to wake up. The sun needs to get back to work.*

I let off the embrace, and the sky returns to the heavens as I return to the earth. When will the two collide again? Maybe never, and this saddens me. But I refuse to show it, and I take off my army issue green coat and cover our heads as we leave the stone gazebo and head back inside the cabin.

That was—mmmmmmm—I will reread that several times today and tomorrow. You make me appreciate the wind. I hope to make you appreciate the rain. Keep your watch loose for me so we can steal a little more time and let the rain trap us for just a bit longer, because sometimes I don't want to return. Someday I would like to touch the ground for just a little while, ten more minutes? Just to look into your eyes and dream. Just to hold your face in my hands and think how perfect, to run my fingers through the back of your hair and soft curls. To hold your hands and marvel at the fingers that write such amazing things that I can't think straight while reading them. The words that only belong to me, the words that make me completely belong to you, if only here on paper, then hopefully in the place we call home. Let me belong to you for just a little while longer.

I **do** *believe in love at first sight, and I'm proof that it's real. I fell in love with you the first time I ever saw you lying in the snow … and here we are today. You are that golden ring on the merry-go-round at the circus and always will be. At least now I've stretched far enough to touch it each time I go around. I may fall off someday trying, but the ring will still be there. It won't fall off unless I get my hands wrapped around it and pull really hard. But I'd need really good balance to do that.*

What we have you will never have to share. Follow your heart and soul, and I will stand by you even if it means losing you. I love writing to you and about you. You bring out the good in me in this terrible place. I wish we could just disappear back to the mountain. The night continues on without you, just me and my thoughts. Which, by the way, are only about you. I look back on the day and can barely remember it. I think about our path to the cabin and how I need to go back up there soon. It will be so lonely without you, but it's a trip I must make I just don't want to abandon you here alone, not even for a day.

I wonder what age sixty-five will be like. Will you remember me? Will we look back at all this and try and figure out how the stars aligned and we were able to connect? If we never again do, will we wonder for eternity? There have been and will be only two women that I will ever love. If the earth is my real life, then you are my sky at sunset. Beautiful, colorful, memorable, never touching the earth and always out of reach. No one will ever be that but you.

I will hold on to these words forever, George. Thank you.

I know that you are not there, but it sure seems like you are. I know you have gone back to the cabin, and while I hope you never have to come back down here, I'm hoping you will. I'm very lonely without you. I sit here and write nonstop to no one but myself, and I keep asking the same questions. Can you change the weather? Can you change the storm that has brewed into our strong path? Then I have to be real, and I have to be alert to what is really going on and not just what I dream about. Every word you write to me is so true. You can't change the weather, but you can tell me to bundle up. Let's not get frustrated with what we can't have. Let's just cherish what we do have. I will try. It's so much more than I could have ever dreamed; now I'm not sure what to do with it. What do I have? Your love … this is the greatest gift of all. I could never ask for more than this, and I guess from today on I need to understand it. I'm searching for words. I want to tell you how special you are, but I've done that so many times I don't want it to lose its effect. How about this? Your smile is the light that guides my direction! It's that nightlight that I sleep to every night. Without that light, at this point in my life and stuck in this camp, I'd be wandering around out in the dark, lost with no direction … and no you. Your love brings fullness to my day, reason to survive this day and the next one. Your smile is heartwarming. I still see the picture in my mind of you smiling and waving. I could look at you all day and still want to look more. I cannot wait until you return from the mountain, as I hope this letter will find you

THE CAMP

George awoke to his own blood spitting out of his heavily swollen mouth. His eyes slowly opened as he fought to see light though his face that seemed just as swollen. There was had dried blood all over his face, and it was tough to tell where hell ended and his face began. He had several cuts on his face, and the blood from those cuts was black as night from several days of drying on his face. His beard had collected dirt and small rocks from the filthy ground on which he'd been lying for a week. His stomach growled for food, as George had not eaten any in days. George wasn't even sure if he could eat anything. His mouth was so numb he didn't even know if he still had teeth.

As the sun cracked through the door, he could hear the sound of scuffling outside. He was not sure what the noise was, but after his last beating he was just hoping they were not coming back for him. This sounded like trucks and tanks on the move more than anything else. George was having a hard time remembering the last time he actually had a visitor. George was beaten and left for dead in the place the prisoners referred to as the hole. He wasn't sure why they grabbed him or why took him to this desolate place, but his spirit was broken.

In the acute German language he actually understood, he was under the impression they were trying to get bombing information out of him. They had assumed that George had jumped out of the plane that crashed some time ago, but they were not sure of his role with the army. George was adamant that he would die before giving up information about his country. When he did not talk, they refused to waste a bullet on him. Instead, they punished him by letting him starve and keeping him locked in the hole. George was starting to get his memory back. He was trying to figure out how long he'd been in here but had no way of knowing. *Was Eve okay?* Thought George as he lay in his premature tomb. He raised his right arm to try and sit up but was quickly jerked back down to the ground by the rusty black chain that was attached to his wrist and locked to a metal loop embedded into the ground. George did not have the desire or the strength to try to pull it out of the ground. He knew it was fruitless effort.

The badly beaten man began to look around the small room. The first thing he noticed was that he had no clothes on. He was shivering but did not realize he was naked because his body was numb from the abuse he endured the past few weeks. The only form of clothing George had, was the wool sweater Eve had made for him. He used the sweater as a pillow for his head, but it was now badly torn and full of dirt rolled up in a corner of the box. The winter months had come and nearly gone, but George had no idea what date or month it really was. He thought life was so bad in the prison that he truly now understood the meaning of hell. *Is this where I'm going to die?* He thought.

The room was dark and hard to see around. Only the glow from the light coming though the crack was his company. The hole was really a wood and metal box, not much bigger than a man himself, which was half buried in the ground. There was no room to stand up and no room to fully lie down. It was truly a nightmare to be trapped inside it. He'd witnessed a number of prisoners die in this box. He recalled when they grabbed him how his friend Fritz could do nothing about it. That was the last time he saw him, standing there as George was dragged away. Fritz just watched with a cold face, as he knew Stone's fate. He didn't want to show any emotion, and he didn't want to feel any emotion. That's what made him a good soldier. What was now most disappointing for Stone was the fact that he didn't have a chance to write a final letter to Eve. If these were to be his final thoughts, no one would share them. This made tears come to his eyes.

"Awe ..." George muttered in pain. If he had not yet gone mad in his time in the box, he was surely about to. Or better yet, he would soon be dead, and all this would be over. The worries of the world would be over—at least for one young American. *What would happen to Eve? Would she be able to move on to a new life? Was she truly the reason I am here? Was she my mission? Would she even remember me? Of course she would! But she would have to move on. This is not the way I want her to remember me. Maybe she'll head back to the cabin and finish our Stone Chapel. Maybe she'll find a new love so she can happily live the rest of her life!* George thought to himself over and over again. That's all there was for him to do—sit and think. He would die soon, and it would all be over. That seemed like a pretty good plan right about now as his stomach was aching like a cancer that had no cure.

He pulled up and leaned closer to the crack in the door to try to squint through it. Something was going on outside. It was a lot of activity. Stone dropped to the ground, and his head painfully slammed into the dirt. Normally that would hurt a man, but George couldn't be hurt anymore on the outside and possibly not on the inside either. His was a soul that was wearing thin. His attrition was just about over, and his body could feel it. His days were down to just a few, and this would be how his life would end. *What will happen to my body? Will they bury me or throw me in a ditch and burn me? Will they care? Will there be compassion for my freshly released soul?* George thought as he started to quietly laugh and chuckle.

"Ha … ha … ha … ha!"

For no reason at all, the young American soldier had just started to laugh, and he did not know why. This confusion just made him laugh even more.

"Haaa … haaa … haaa!"

George started to laugh out of control, and his stomach, bones, and face were all starting to hurt in unison. This made him laugh even harder!

"What a life! What a situation! How in God's name did I ever end up here? And look how it's all going to end? I'm naked in a wooden box! I'm insane with love for a woman that may not still be alive or will never see me again! My body will soon be tossed into a ditch and burned! My best friend is dead, my family thinks I'm dead, and they will never know the truth! My country is at war, and I am not able to help in any way! I'm naked in a box, and I don't know what month it is! Ha … ha … ha!" George continued to laugh at loud as he began yelling from inside the box.

"I was in a plane crash, and I was the only one who survived! I found paradise only to lose it because I was hunting for food to survive and someone heard the shots! I found true love in the last place on earth I ever expected to find it, and I will never be allowed to explore it! I had my face beat in just because of the country that I'm from! I'm twenty something years old from a small town in Kansas and I'm *naked in a box!*" George yelled and laughed at the same time. Stone's lungs were now once again working to full strength, and he was actually starting to feel better inside. The yelling and laughing was good for his mind and his soul.

Meanwhile outside the box, two soldiers jumped off a jeep because they thought they heard a voice … moreover, they thought they had heard laughter. The voice appeared to be American. The two looked at each other and walked quietly to investigate. Despite the sounds of trucks and tanks roaring by and soldiers marching in pattern, the two seemed determined to find the distant laughter. The camp was empty. Everyone here had either been killed or let out of the gate … everyone except this voice that was growing louder. The two soldiers stumbled upon the box that was half buried in the ground. Only the door and the top of the square shaped box stuck out. The American voice was ringing out of the box, and the soldiers were desperate to find it.

Inside the box George suddenly heard someone pounding on it. *Oh God they're back!* He thought. *They've come to kill me!*

George was a little concerned at first but then was at peace with his destiny. He quietly sat up and awaited their arrival. Moments later the door ripped open as one of the soldiers used an axe to break the lock.

"You okay in there?" yelled an American voice. George was taken back a bit. The sun suddenly exploded from a small crack in a door to a full white out as his eyes tried to adjust to the light.

"You okay, buddy?" The second soldier asked as he bent down and held out his canteen. "You need some water?" George quickly grabbed the silver and metal round gift from God and began to pour it all over his mouth and face. His right hand was still chained to the ground, but his left hand took charge as the water soaked his long and dirty hair, rock-filled beard, and badly swollen eyes. The water cleaned the dirt that was in his eyes, and he could clearly see that two young American soldiers were kneeling in front of the box.

"Let's get you out of here, buddy!" one said as they fumbled through a large ring with keys on it before eventually finding the right one. The caged prisoner reached his arm out to the soldiers, and one of the men stuck the key in the hole of the chain and clicked it off George's wrist. His arm was red with blood and purple from bruises that were reminders of the intense beatings he had endured. George reached back and grabbed his old dirty and torn wool sweater and put it under his arm. He did not want to leave this precious item in the hole. Both soldiers grabbed him by the arm and slid him out of the box. George was very weak and needed to be carried as he was pulled from the small hell he'd lived in.

"Here, take this!" The first soldier took off his jacket that covered his beige and white uniform and put it around George's naked body as they tried to get him to his feet.

"How long have you been in that box?" he asked in amazement while covering George with the jacket.

"I don't know," George answered. "What is this? Where are the German soldiers?"

"You're free, friend! The Germans abandoned this camp three days ago. We forced them out from the south and drove them back. They fled, and you're officially back on French land now, friend," the soldier explained with a smile and an arm around George's shoulder. As Stone struggled to walk, he pulled the jacket down a little closer to his waist, trying to hide the embarrassment of not wearing any clothes. He looked around the camp trying to see if Eve was anywhere around, but he did not see her. What he did see was almost as good.

There were American troops all over the camp walking around the building looking for other survivors or other forms of life in the camp. He looked out onto the road and the fleet of U. S. tanks and trucks and jeeps lined the road as far as the eye could see. He also looked up to the hills wondering what had become of the cabin and their Stone Chapel. There was no way to see it or tell exactly where it was located, but he wondered what had become of Eve and if she was still up there. The thoughts were beginning to overtake his mind. His recent energy surge had taken just about all the battery he had left inside for this day. George Stone was so exhausted he collapsed into the arms of the soldiers. The two men carried him to a stretcher and laid him down on it. An American doctor in full military uniform walked up to him and began to check his vital signs. He put his hand on Stone's wrist to check his pulse. The doctor then forced open George's eyes to check his pupils, but Stone was now off into slumber.

"Looks like we got a live one, boys. Nice work!" offered the doctor. The two American soldiers smiled and then turned and walked off in search of other prisoners while the doctor motioned to two other soldiers.

"Come here and get him on the truck. We need to get an IV into him and get this brave man back to the plane and off to London. Let's move it."

The three men grabbed his wooden stretcher, as George lay motionless in a deep sleep. They picked it up by the rails and moved it toward the truck just behind them. As they slowly set the small temporary bed onto the edge of the truck, George's left arm slid off his body and fell over the side, hitting the back of the truck. The small jolt to his arm forced a dislodging of the homemade, small, metal woven ring that was around his finger. The ring slid off and danced as it fell to the ground. None of the men noticed the small ring's leap to the ground, but one man did grab his arm and swing it back onto his chest. They pushed George into the back of the truck as the prized ring lay softly on the ground.

The men hopped up into the back of the clearly marked U. S. Red Cross cargo truck and pulled it away out of the camp. The big tires began to roll and turn and slowly pull away from the small metal ring that lay silent near the gate.

George would never see the ring again but would often wonder what happened to it.

THE LETTERS

Boo, I got up early today and walked down to the fence, but no letter. I hope you are okay …

Okay, day two and no letter. Where are you? My God, I hope you are still there. I've looked for Fritz, but I can't seem to find him to give him my letter.

It's been a week, and no letter and no sign of you either. You were right; it really is a tragedy. I don't think I can handle this. I fear something horrible has happened to you. Still, I continue to write this letter hoping someday I will find a way to give it to you. I hope and pray every day that you are still alive

This will be my final letter at the gate. It's been days and no sign of you. I can tell there is movement inside the camp, but I'm not sure what is going on. I watch for hours but no you. Where are you? Where is Fritz? I will leave these unread letters under this rock hoping that someday you will find them. I've will write the name Stone on the rock and hopefully you will see it. I'm heading back to the cabin again for fear of danger in this area. I hope to someday return and find you. I also feel the need to return to Dover. It's been several years now, and I need to know what has happened to that town. I pray every day that we will see each other one more time, but I fear that you are dead. I fear that you are somewhere standing in a field of yellow flowers waiting for me. I can't think of any other reason you have not written me back or are not standing by the gate waiting for me to walk by. I trust in us, and I know that you would be there if you could. I hope this is not good-bye, but I fear it is. I cry every night wondering why I can't see you or read your words. I guess I should be thankful for the time we shared at the cabin. It was brief but something I wouldn't change for the world. You saved my life in more ways than one, and I have no way of telling you thank you. I will keep the ring you made and the name you offered to me. I will always keep our Stone Chapel as long as I live. Keep making me proud. I'll miss you, and even if I can never contact you again, I'm me and you are you and you are inside of me, so I will have you always.

End of the line.

*There **must** be something in the wind that may always keep a wedge between us. Our timing has been the worst. Everything is a just miss, and I can't figure* *out why. I'm writing this letter from a hospital bed in London, and I'm sure you will never read it. I kept looking for you just to see you from a distance, but at the end of the line you were not there. I know this was not your fault, and I know that you probably returned to see me and I was already gone. Now I wonder if you think I'm dead.*

*Our talk time was limited, but every moment of it is recorded in my mind. This is a conversation I'll be thinking about in my brain at age ninety-five. People will be looking at me, and I'll be all alone talking to myself and staring off into space. They'll say, "I wonder what's going on in that old man's head?" It will be thoughts of you. Hopes and dreams I know will never have come true over my life but a part of it I will never forget. I promise you this ... I will return to the cabin at least two more times in my life. The first will be as soon as I'm healthy enough for travel and they let me return. I will try to find you ... that I promise. If I don't I will accept it and let both of our souls move on. But I **will** return again. I may be fifty or sixty, but I will return to the cabin. I don't think I could live my life without knowing what happened to you.*

Those are the two promises I give to you, the woman I love. No matter what you will always be in my heart, and I mean that. I'm in London now, but they will be sending me home soon. The war is about over, and while I've asked to be sent back to Calais, they have denied my request. Once the war is over, they will evacuate all American soldiers and return the country to the French people. I don't even know why I'm writing this letter, I know you will never get it. I don't even know how to get it to you. I wonder what happened to Fritz. He proved that people are good and can make the right choices.

I wonder if we will ever be together again. Maybe it was my destiny just to let you know that someone out there was willing to risk it all for you. Just to let you know that you are not alone in this world and that you are loved for whatever the decisions you make. Maybe that is why I was chosen and lucky enough to meet you and get to spend the time with you I did. What will the future hold? I just don't know! Is it my place to try and find you after all this time or should I just let it be? I write my feelings 'cause I don't know how to say them. Was this just one of those crazy things that happens and now we are back to the real world, or is there a woman still waiting for me back at our Stone Chapel? I have to let time decide. You think I'm dead, and you've probably moved on because of it. If I re-enter your life will I be destroying something I was able to help save? I have to make a decision and stick by it. I must choose the future right now. Maybe it's true—maybe the words that I'm about to write are the correct ones. I only pray they are because if you are waiting for me and I never find you again, what a horrible mistake I will have made.

Part 7

THE MOUNTAIN
1953

The trip down the mountain certainly was an easier trip than the one back up it! George thought as he continued to move forward up the familiar mountain. Adding to the difficult arch was the weather and miles of deep snow. The last time George was on this big hill, it was early summer, and he was flying down it carrying an injured woman in search of a doctor. George knew the risk he was taking back then but thought the outcome would be worth it. Even though he suffered immense physical pain, he knew he made the right decision taking Eve into town. He thought he could fake his way out of a tight situation. Moreover, he thought he could talk his way out of a bad situation.

Neither occurred, and George found himself locked behind a barbed wire fence for the next several months. The woman he loved and saved for a second time was on the outside of the fence looking in. Both were helpless to rectify the situation. However, they both had the memories of the cabin, the hidden, old, private cabin. It became the true home to the life that he remembered. George knew that no matter what happened after his imprisonment and no matter what happened after the war, he would meet Eve at this special place.

Only thing was George never got a chance to say good-bye. He never got a chance to tell the woman he loved that he was being shipped off. They came in like angels from the sky and plucked him from his death hole and rushed him off to safety. What had happened to his English girl? George did not know. Did she even know he was still alive? These were the questions that had rolled through his head every night for eight years. It had been nearly a decade, and the travel restrictions to this country had just been lifted, giving him permission to reenter. The world was finally safe for travel again, and it was time for him to make his journey. Eight painful years had passed, and George had no way of contacting his past life that had meant so much to him. That is what made this solo journey so important. This rite of passage allowed by his government had a meaning and a destination: the cabin George hoped held all the answers to his questions. He knew his journey would be a long one, and he knew the result could be a painful one. But he had to take this chance to get closure … to find resolution to many unanswered questions. The cabin would provide this—as would seeing the woman he loved. She must have left him a note or a sign—something to help him locate her, he just knew it.

The wind picked up a little as George continued to stomp his big black boots through the snow. The sun was out, so it was not as cold as it could have been. For this George was thankful. But a warm fire in the cabin would soothe his pain both physically and mentally. He wore a padded cap to protect his head, heavy gloves to protect his hands, and heavy trousers to keep his temperature normal. His heavy winter mountain-ready jacket protected his torso, but the wool sweater that peeked out around his neck protected his heart. It was the same sweater that she had made for him nine years earlier, and though it had been torn in several spots inside the camp, he never abandoned it. In fact, after he returned to London, he cleaned it and sewed most of the holes back up, and then proudly wore the sweater. It was all that he had to remind him of her and he always kept it close.

The wool sweater had been mended many times, but his heart was still in need of a good stitching. Several times he had considered abandoning the whole idea of coming back. The last few months held horrible memories for him, and the only thing that had gotten him through the days were the letters and the one kind guard that would quickly exchange the notes through the fence with Eve. George still was not sure what ever happened to his friend Fritz. Was he shot or maybe dead? Probably so, but it was the guard who saved George. Had it not been for the notes exchanged through the fence, George would have surely died inside the prison. When a man has no hope, he has no reason to live. George had hope and a very strong reason to live, but what happened to his dream? This he did not know but set out to discover the answer. That was why he was making this journey, and that was why this was so important.

The snow seemed to get thicker and deeper with every step he took. George looked down and noticed a long, skinny stick, so he reached down and grabbed it. The weight from his bright orange backpack nearly tipped him over as he reached for it. He put his glove-covered hands on it and pulled it up. George was now twenty-nine years old, and although he did not need the walking stick to move through the snow, he did need a companion, and the stick served this purpose. Just then the wind whipped by his face as if to say hello or welcome back—George wasn't really sure. But the colder he got the more comfortable he got. He was getting closer to home. It was still over a mile away, but it was as close as George had been to home … his real home … in nearly ten years.

He stopped walking and looked up the mountain. His hand reached up and pulled the tinted goggles off his face. This movement unveiled his dark blue eyes surrounded by the red sunburn that was starting to chap his face. George glanced around looking for any signs of smoke. Smoke would mean fire, and fire would mean people. His cabin was pretty far away, but if people were living in it, they would need a fire on a day like today. George did not see smoke. He sadly pulled the glasses back down over his eyes and continued his journey up the mountain.

LATER THAT DAY

It was the snow-covered roof that first caught George's eye as he came walking over the final hill before the distant cabin.

It was exactly how he remembered it, and he got a very warm and comforting feeling in his heart. It was no bigger than a small shack in the woods, smaller than he'd remembered, but to him it was larger than life. For George this was his life! This was the reason he took a breath every day, and this was the reason he had fought so hard to survive in the prison. This distant home that had been so far away was now just a few footsteps from him.

The closer he got to the cabin the more he realized this was exactly how he remembered it in his dreams and in real life. It was summer the last time he left this mountain; how fitting after the last few months of hardship here that it was now winter.

George's view was like a beautiful painting on a canvas that few ever had the wonderful opportunity to see in person. The cabin was just one room, but from the outside it looked like heaven would look if he were allowed to peek in. The cabin sat on a drift of snow, or at least it appeared that way. Trees, like arrows stuck headfirst in the ground, surrounded nearly three-fourths of the cabin. Their leaves had long since turned yellow and fallen off, and some were now bare, but they continued to line the cabin as if to protect it from the damaging sun in the summer and from the wind and ice in the winter. Yes, this palace of solitude was in the perfect location. The wood logs that made up the outside of the cabin were a little more gray than George remembered but still appeared to be in good condition. To the south sat one faded red door, and George noticed that slightly down the hill from the front of the cabin were three graves all in a row. They had long since been covered in rough brown grass and snow. Only the crosses of wood peeking up from the white covered graves were noticeable. George knew exactly what they were and who they were. They were the three soldiers he had killed the last time he'd stepped on this mountain soil; someone had buried them not far from the cabin.

As he approached, George noticed that door appeared to be slightly open, possibly blown by the wind. George recalled that this had happened several times while he was in the cabin. The door never seemed to shut all the way. Above that door was the only window in the cabin, and while the glass was still intact, there appeared to be some damage to the wood on each side of the window. It was clear to George that no one was or had been living in this cabin for some time. As he got closer, he noticed the wind that had been blowing earlier began to drift off a bit and the sun was quickly fading to the east. This would be his home at least tonight because this weather made for scary travel after dark. Plus, it was nearly a half a day's walk back down the hill ... although George had once made it in less than an hour driving a truck.

George walked up to the red faded door and stopped a few feet away from the entrance. This was what he had been dreaming about the last eight years. He was a little unsure of what he might find or whom he might find. He looked around at the surrounding dagger-like trees that stood neatly forty feet into the sky. He noticed that the grass that had not died or been covered by snow was quite long. It had been several years since someone occupied this home, perhaps no one since him and Eve all those years ago. This feeling made him smile and also supplied the confidence he needed to continue on inside the small cabin.

George put his hand on the knob then pulled back and pushed the door the rest of the way open. The room was dark, but George could see, thanks to the distant retiring sun casting a final glow into the room. Snow had made its way into the cabin in several places, and he would have to fix the door if he was going to spend the night. For a second—just a split second—George could feel warmth in the room ... then he was cold again. He slowly began panning the room from left to right as the sun crept in around the edges of the south door and the wall joints. The room was exactly how he remembered it. The table where he ate many home-cooked meals was to his left. Every day it was his job to go out and hunt for food. He would bring it back and together George and Eve would prepare the dinner. Then to candlelight, they would eat the dinner as they stared into each other's eyes. This legacy had grown in his mind over the years. The table was worn, and the red and white cover on the floor was covered in dirt and snow. Behind the table was the cabinet. It was just as worn with dirt and dust as the wood on the table and the metal framing that lined the doors. This cabinet was where he'd kept his rifle. He had taught Eve how to use it just in case the worst should happen, but it turned out she already knew how to use a rifle. Her father had taught her that many years earlier. He'd kept his army side pistol and ammunition inside the upright wooden box as well. He was curious if they were still there.

Although the cabin was well worn by the weather, the inside living area did not appear to be disturbed. There was even a huge salad bowl lying on the floor next to the table that George recognized. He looked on top of the cabinet and saw three circular canisters that held the film from his camera.

He quickly remembered his job with the army was Stars and Stripes. He was a news photojournalist. His job was to shoot video of the war and get it back for all those newsreels in the states. His mission had been interrupted. That thought made him smile a bit. His camera sat quietly next to the film canisters on the top of the cabin.

As George panned the logs that lined the wall, he noticed the cement that held the logs together and lined the walls was also in good shape. The inside was much more red and brown in color than the outside. George was unsure if this was the glow of the sun or the color of the walls. On the floor lay several bowls and bottles and even a vase for flowers. The wind had blown all this to the floor. The fireplace was full of cobwebs but appeared to be ready to host a fire.

A fire was in George's plans, but first he would have to locate some wood. The fireplace was always one of his favorite things about this small heaven. It was stone from top to bottom and would live long past the time of the wood logs and this lifetime that George was living. George always respected the builder of this cabin because it was way ahead of its time and was built with extra strength in the walls. The double-stacked wood logs gave this cabin life and protection from the outside elements. It was truly the cornerstone of the cabin. Next to the fireplace was a ladder that ascended to the loft that was the bedroom. George would not be sleeping up there tonight; that was a special place. Plus, from the outside, George knew that the room had already been breached by the weather. A small end table was next to the ladder, and the porcelain bowl and water pitcher were still sitting on top of it. How ironic that the bowl and pitcher that were used for hygiene were in fact themselves dirty and full of dust. A lantern hung from the ceiling right above the table and while George was positive it was out of kerosene. That was okay because he had brought some in his backpack.

Two chairs lay on their backs next to the table. Two others stood upright near the front door. There was a wood rocking chair in the room as well. All the way to the right was a small twin bed. George remembered this bed well. He'd made the frame out of some logs and the bed from some hay and twine; Eve had contributed by sewing the mattress together. They had decided to make it a bigger bed so if their family ever expanded they could grow into it. George had no idea how long they would live in the cabin but would have gladly given his final breath in it if his family could have been with him. That did not happen. While this was beginning to make George a little sad, he quickly got a calm feeling, as he now knew where he would be sleeping tonight.

His first goal was to find some wood and get a fire going; second, to clean and seal the doors to preserve the room; third, to pull out a can of beans and cook them in the fire. The trip had made George very hungry. As he reached around and pulled off his backpack, he set it on the twin bed and began to look around again. Nothing was new. Nothing was different. Was this a bad sign? Was there a clue for him to discover here in this place? He would begin his search later. Right now it was getting dark and he needed wood. He turned, opened the door and began his journey for firewood. His eight years of questions would have to wait at least another hour.

LATER THAT NIGHT

The wind whistled as it worked its way through the wall joints and the loft upstairs. George lay quietly in the twin size bed he'd made several years earlier. His back was propped up by the backpack he'd been wearing all day. The room was much warmer than when he first entered, and the flames from the fire he'd built were slowing receding into ash. A small flicker from time to time would light up George's face from across the room. The only true light was from a distant lamp illuminating the room. It swayed slightly as the wind altered its hanging flow. George sat quietly and listened to the soft wind as he continued to put thoughts back into his mind. They were pleasant thoughts of several years ago in this very place—memories of Eve and the time they spent here.

George recalled lying with his favorite person in nearly this same position as she sat behind him rubbing his neck. He softly rubbed her womb that was starting to grow like their love had in a very short period of time. He remembered how she would run her fingers along the back on his neck and how they would continue up through his hair. Oh, how he loved that feeling; that was his favorite memory of her. He also had bad memories of their time here, but he refused to let those thoughts enter his mind on this night. *I know she's been here. She would have come back and left me something, I just know it,* he thought to himself.

George continued to scan the room that was now much cleaner than it was just a couple of hours before. Even the dirty red and white tablecloth had been picked up, cleaned, and put back on the table. The bowl was back in its rightful place atop the table. The porcelain bowl and pitcher were cleaned off as well, and warm water was now in the bowl. George prepared the room as if he was expecting a visitor. Yet no visitor came. *She would have left me a note or something. Even if she'd thought I was dead she would have left me something just in case I was alive,* he thought.

His eyes eventually made their way back to the cabinet that was sitting next to the fireplace. He had cleaned everywhere except there. His mind had wandered and he had forgotten to look to see if his rifle and pistol were still inside. He kicked his feet off the side of the bed and stood up. He took the coffee cup that he'd been softly holding and set it on the table as he walked over to the cabinet. Dust dominated the wood structure as he leaned in and blew some off the doors. Then he reached down and grabbed the small wooden knobs and opened the two metal-lined doors. There inside was his rifle. Next to it hung his pistol. George had left the rifle lying on the floor next to the soldiers he had killed some years earlier. But Eve apparently picked it up and cleaned it off.

George raised an eyebrow as he noticed one glaring thing. Neither was dusty. They had both been cleaned recently. Maybe not this year or maybe not last, but the condition of the rifle and the pistol were supreme to anything else in this cabin.

"She was here!" George said proudly. *But there has to be more … a note … something!* He wondered. George began to rustle through the cabinet looking for something; any sign of Eve, but there was nothing. He went through the cabinet again and again. He grabbed his small metal film canister box and opened the lid. To his surprise there were all the notes and letters he had written her, as well as the letters he had returned to her folded up inside the small box. He pulled them out a couple at a time and looked them over. He could not control the joy he was feeling as he laughed just a little. He put the letters back in the metal box as if to save this special treat for later and then set it back down and continued on his mission.

George stood puzzled for a second and then glared up at his three film canisters and camera that sat inside the cabinet. The film was surely bad by now, and the camera was so dusty that it was probably damaged, but he noticed another interesting item. The three other circular canisters were sitting up a bit higher than he seemed to remember. He looked a little closer and noticed a small, paper-like item under the canisters. He reached up and pulled them from the shelf and set them inside next to his rifle. As he pulled the final one up and set it down inside the cabinet, he realized this was a picture, and it was not one that he had left.

His rough fingers slid across the top of the photo that was stuck to the wood. He used part of his fingernail to work the picture up as to not damage it. He pulled it to his face and his heart fell. George began to get a feeling in his soul he hadn't known for several years. He fought back tears as long as he could, but there was no stopping this. In the picture was young girl. The child appeared to three or four years old. She was by herself with no mother in the background. *This was a picture meant just for me,* he thought as it was placed in a spot where he would probably be the only one to discover it. His mission was accomplished.

George took a few steps back and softly slid down into the rocker sitting behind him. The fire had turned a darker shade of orange, and the flicking was much more intense on his face since he was closer to it. George continued to look at the picture. He knew that Eve thought he was dead. At that moment the past eight years came to realization in George's mind.

After he was put into the hole and lost contact with her, Eve surely thought he must have been killed. Then even after he was discovered and the prison camp was cleaned out so quickly, she must have thought he was dead because he never came for her.

She must have looked around time and time again for a note or something that told her to wait, something that told her there was hope. George had not left anything. There was no time, and he was not in control of his departure. His ring had somehow fallen off his finger, but he wasn't sure where it was. Maybe she had found it and thought it was the signal to her that he had not survived. He knew this was why she left the picture where she did. She knew that he would return here someday if he were alive and that this picture would be his reward. But what kind of a reward was she leaving? This could not be his child—she wasn't old enough. George did not know when the picture was taken, but Eve surely was not pregnant when he was in the camp.

Or was she? He asked himself. *Wouldn't she have told me?* He was beginning to understand why she did not leave him a note or anything other than the picture. She gave him some time, but she had to move on. *How long would she wait?* He wondered. George feared in his heart that she had long since given up and created a life with someone else. It had been more than eight years, eight long years, and no word. Surely she must have come to this spot several times, always cleaning his gun so he would know this. But the girl in this picture could not have been more than five or six years old. She was small and looked very young. *This picture could have been at least two to three years old. Was she still waiting? If so, why was this cabin in the shape it was in? Did she want everything to stay the same as it was? Would she be back? How long could I wait for her?* These were the questions that George asked himself as he stared at the picture of the young girl. Maybe this is a final farewell picture from Eve letting George know that she had moved on. This one final note was in the form of a picture that did not include her or a new family, so George would not be hurt if he were to see it.

"I wonder what your name is," he stated to the motionless picture as he held it in between his fingers that had started to sweat. That's when he decided to stay … at least for a little while. He loved this place, and it needed some work. Maybe he could spend some time here fixing the place up and repairing all the damage that the weather and time had done. Maybe the smoke from the fire would penetrate the countryside as a signal letting everyone know that he was back. *Yes, that's my plan, I will stay,* he thought to himself. Maybe he would also make a trip down the mountain and back across the channel to Dover; maybe that's where he would find his answer.

George leaned back in the chair and put his feet up on the table.

"How long can I stay?" he argued with himself. "How long can my heart take this? How long will it take before I give up?"

He set the picture down on the table, not knowing if he would ever meet this little girl or if he would ever see Eve again, but he knew he had come too far to quit. If she had moved on, he would discover this over time and stay out of her life so he would not cause her pain. If not, maybe the gods would finally turn his way. It was a tough decision but one George was willing to make. He would wait for now and cross a new bridge if a new one was presented to him ... that was his plan. It was a good plan.

THE ATTIC ...

Maybe true love is what you make it. Maybe the love we think we feel is just a relaxation of the brain. Maybe the world we live in and the world we build for ourselves becomes that love that the soul so desperately craves.

My father used to swear that everyone in the world saw colors differently. What might be red to me was green to him. What I saw as yellow was his white. How different our worlds would look if we could see them through the eyes of another. How different faces would look, smiles, frowns, and cheers. The world we live in would be a completely different place. Like the colors, maybe our thoughts would revel the same way. What feels like love to me is hate to another? What feels like need to me is meaningless to another. Maybe this can truly be the answer to all we know about each other ... we know nothing about each other until we live others lives, seen their thoughts, and understood their dreams. These are the real issues that occupy the space that sits on our shoulders ... and I think my father truly understood them. He knew what was within reach and what was not. He knew where he stood and how to cross any path that was in front of him because everything was going the same direction. Sometimes you had to step over a path or from one path to another to get there, but he knew. We are all going the same place, but who among us would truly enjoy, envision, and understand the journey that it will take to get there? This my father understood.

The long sleep awaits us all. The attrition of the soul is our destiny. The final acceptance of rest will overcome everyone eventually, so enjoy what you have while you have it. Soon it will be gone and another flower will grow in its place making all that came after ... forget the once-mighty seed. This my father understood.

Those who could not rest would never have the answers to the questions they were asking. Take what you are given and be free with your decisions. Know that some questions are better left unanswered because they will never be understood. The answers do not exist because the question is the answer. Why do we live a life of love and loss? Why not? Can love truly be lost anyway? Look up and look around. Love is what you have. Love is what will have you. That's the true meaning of the word. When you lose that, you lose everything. We will all lose everything someday, but today we have everything we need. This my father understood.

He died on a blustery November day. It was the seventeenth when they found his body lying in a field that blossomed into a beautiful golden patch of sunflowers every summer. There were no proud flowers this day, just thousands of broken stems covered in snow. They said he died of exposure, although he was fighting colon cancer. Due to his brittle state, the cancer eventually won the fight. I think that's why he went to that field, because he knew he would never see it bloom again. I feel he actually died several years earlier. It was not exposure or cancer that took his life, but rather an exhausted soul. A lonely heart can put someone in a grave many years ahead of his time. And while he may continue to walk the earth, it's the sunset where he really lives.

I was not present when he passed, but I would like to think he saw the color blue the same way as I do. Soft, yet strong and powerful like the ocean. Shy, yet radiantly bright like the sky on a sunny day, beautiful … like the eyes of a goddess passing by your view. His blue had to look the same as mine. Nothing is so perfect as the color blue. He used to say, "Look at the sunset just before dusk. The clouds appear to look like mountains topping a lake. It's a canvas in the sky." He would tell us, "That's God's way of showing you how beautiful heaven is."

He used to tell me a nighttime story that I never really appreciated until I read his final long, sad letter. It was the story of a young man who fought for everything in life that he wanted. It was a story of courage and bravery, at least what I could remember before my eyelids became too heavy to stay open. It was a story about how a young man's life could change and how one little smile could lead to a lifetime of love and learning. His story could flow on some nights, at least the ones that I could fall asleep to. He told of a fairy tale of a man and woman who fell in love but soon lost it. The man traveled thousands of hard miles to find the woman he lost, only to discover that she had moved on. Her attrition had run out long before, and she started another family based on the love she had found in him. The story went on about a young man who learned how to love and used his relationship as a foundation to build a stronger one later in life. I see now this was my father telling me about his life and how one young love helped him grow into the one he had with my mother.

His bedtime story usually wrapped up with this young man walking through an old English town and seeing this woman from a distance with her small young daughter. The woman did not see him, but he would tell just how happy she was with her new child and the new family she had made. The young man wanted more than anything to walk up and give her a hug, but he knew this was not meant for him. His time was over, and anything he did to make contact with the woman would only hurt her new life. The only way he could truly love her was to never talk to her again. The story did have a happy ending, however. The young man returned home and met a second wonderful woman later in life who fulfilled all his dreams as well. This love was based on what he had learned from his first love endured.

"That's a long story!" I'd tell him on the nights that I somehow stayed awake through it all. He would laugh and then put me to bed. As he walked to the door of my room, my mother would be standing there, smiling and waiting for her man to finish his story. It was one she had heard several times as well. She understood his story because somewhere in her past she had a story of her own. We all do. They would hug and kiss, then flip off my lights as I dozed off to sleep. That was a good night, and I never really understood the meaning of it until now. My father was a quiet man, and he never openly discussed his past—at least not his emotional past. I knew he had spent time in prison during the war, but I never knew the extent of it. He was a quiet man. He was a good man. And now I wish I could thank Eve for it.

My father is now on his mountain and from time to time he grabs his fishing pole and heads down to that lake. He hopes to catch dinner, for his love that awaits him in the cabin. It's their home now. A home they finally share together. It's their love they now have for eternity.

I grabbed the final letter and gently placed it back into the metal box. Tomorrow I will pull the rest of the trash out of the attic and drag it to the backyard. Then I will strike a match and burn the trash, ridding the world of this mess. Tomorrow I will also take the box of letters down to the fire. I'll pull them in one by one and slowly drop each into the blaze. The letters will burn with such a sweet blue flame that even my father will be proud. He will know that his story is over. He will know that this eternity now truly belongs to him. This story and these memories will have closure and will have a meaning. They will become the ashes that we all become in this place we call home.

If the earth is my real world, then you are my sky at sunset, beautiful, never touching the earth and always out of reach.

The attrition of the soul is over.

My attrition, though, is just beginning. As it turns out, I have a half sister somewhere in this beautiful world. I will make it a goal over the remaining years of my life to find her and maybe her mother. Maybe I can find a way to honor my father and let them know just how much he really loved them. My attrition has just begun.

Part 8

His Return
Calais, France
1986

The strong walls of this small cabin still stood. George Stone was about to complete his final promise to the woman he had fallen in love with forty years earlier. Time passed, yet this place still stood the test of time. George felt very sad as he looked at the old quiet cabin. So much had happened in such a short period of time here, and so much had happened since. George was now an old man, some sixty-two years old. He was recently diagnosed with life's great affliction—an incurable disease. His water line was near the end of the pipes and soon someone else would take his place on this dirt. George had few regrets from his long life. He had been blessed with a wonderful, loving wife he lost several years back. He had a son and a daughter who had made him proud. He'd even been able to make a name for himself as an award-winning author. But his one true regret was standing in front on him in living color and beauty.

George returned to this place one other time, and that's when he discovered what was his was no more. George spent time at the cabin, but no one ever came to visit him. He traveled back to the town that had held him captive, and while it had been rebuilt, his love was still in ruins. He traveled well across the channel to the small town of Dover in search of his love but did not have much success early on. Then, on a bright and sunny day standing outside the deli in Dover and carefully thumbing through a sandwich, his luck changed. He saw his true love walking in front of him. She was as beautiful as the moment he'd left her and was dressed in newer, cleaner clothes than he remembered. She was in an all-white Sunday dress and walking as if she was gliding on the air. She was healthy and smiling.

George could not wait to step out and greet her for the first time in eight years. He turned and dropped the sandwich into a garbage can. He had just lost his appetite and was suddenly craving something else. He turned and was ready to walk to his love when from across the street he noticed a young girl walking behind her. It was the young woman from the photo he had seen in the cabin. George did not know what to do, so he slowly walked alongside her on the other side of the road as she passed. The daughter was nearly as small as she was in the picture. That led George to believe she was not more than five or six years old. This was devastating for Stone, because he knew he'd been gone for too long and there was no way the young girl was his daughter. He continued to follow, not knowing if he should cross the street and reintroduce himself to her. If he did it, would be the greatest journey he'd ever made and his emotions would run at an all-time high. *But what if Eve was now with another man? What if she was married and had tried to put me behind her? This might be devastating to her. My God, her daughter looks just like her!* He thought. This woman he had loved so much had apparently moved on and started a new life. Any attempt at contact by Stone might ruin that for her.

The woman and her daughter continued down the street and eventually walked up to the church. George followed. A man was standing outside and quickly approached the gate as she arrived. George came to a stop across the street and recognized the young man as the second French priest from the church where George had dropped Eve off after she was shot. Only the man was not a priest—at least he wasn't dressed like one on this day. George wasn't sure what to think. He continued to watch closely as his hands and arms began to shake uncontrollably. He had not been this nervous since he killed the three enemy soldiers at the cabin. Killing was something he did then but vowed he would never do again.

Eve walked up to the man now wearing a gray suit and tie and reached over the fence … giving him a big hug and a kiss on the cheek. George's heart fell as he realized this was her new family. The man reached back over the fence and picked up the little girl and gave her a kiss while holding her in his arms. This was too much for George to take. His head dropped as he turned and began walking back the way he'd come. All these miles he'd traveled, and he was too late. The woman he loved and he'd come to find, was already found by another man. She must have thought George was dead and that was why she moved on without him. *Maybe this life I am living is the true gift. Maybe seeing her with a child and in the arms of another man was the mission that was originally designed for me. Maybe my love for her was for her health and I was to be more of a guardian angel than a lover. Maybe I went too far and this was the way it was supposed to be.*

George stopped and turned back to catch one last glimpse of Eve. This was decision time. Go to her now or turn and walk away forever. *Let her think that you have passed and all the memories she has of you now will be there forever. She will always love you for the man that you were and the brief life you spent together. If you go to her now, you risk everything that she has built trying to get over you.* Eve meant too much to George to ever ruin what she had built on her own. They lived and loved together for what seemed like such a very short period of time, but it was probably more love then most people get in their whole lifetime. Sadly, he made his decision to turn and walk. The only way to truly love her now was to never talk to her again. This was his choice. If only he had gotten closer to her, he would have noticed his small metal ring was still woven around her finger. That was the only ring she would ever wear in her lifetime.

So the sixty-two-year-old man stood outside this cabin he had grown to love. His hair was gray all over and balding in spots on the backside of his head. He wore a light jacket, although it was summer and he didn't really need it. He remembered the cold winter air whistling around, and every memory he had of this place involved the cold. That is why he wore the jacket. At his age he could never make it back up the mountain in the wintertime, so he planned his trip now. He wanted to go inside the cabin, but this time he was not looking for anything. Still, he had questions that would never be answered. His remaining family did not even know he was making this trip. He'd just packed up and left telling them he was going out of town. George was still very private even in his tender years.

After his last trip here, he still saw her face for many years to come. It was not until his first child, a young boy, when she really began to fade for him. The letters he had taken back home with him the first time kept him company for many years. They too would end up in a small metal box up in the attic. It was a memory that he did not want to erase but knew he had to get out of his mind. So he wrote his long sad letter and tried to put it all behind him. His new wife had stumbled upon his letter one night and didn't really know what to think. They talked about it and decided it was in his best interest to write it out and put it behind him, and that is exactly what he did. Her love for George was just as strong as Eve's, and she was always very supportive of her husband. It was till death do us part for George, and while the first woman he loved thought he was dead, his current companion would be around for some time. He loved her just as much and while maybe it didn't grow from the same seed, the plant became every bit as big and beautiful as the first one. He made a life with his wife and up until her death;

she was the love of his life. After she passed, he was hurt and his heart began to open in other directions. His family was there for him, and he began to write about her as well. His stories of earned love and lifelong partnerships won him several writing awards, yet inside he had one last promise to fulfill. So he made this trip back to the mountain for the last time. And it was time to go inside the cabin one last time.

George walked up to the cabin door and put his hand on the knob that he'd turned several hundred times before. He knew the door would not be locked because it would only lock if someone were inside to lock it. He turned the knob and gently pushed the door open. To his amazement, the place was a wreck. A part of the roof had caved in, and the weather had spent several years terrorizing the inside of this cabin. It was very clear from where he stood that no one had occupied this space in many, many years. The afternoon sun was shining down through the open roof and lighting the room in all directions. He looked to his left and noticed the old wooden rocking chair was broken and lying under the partially collapsed roof. The side window was broken and it appeared as though animals lived in here from time to time. The table was still sturdy, but it was badly damaged and warped by the weather. The wood on the top was also beginning to crack. The wooden cabinets were lying on their side and splintered as they touched the floor. The ladder that reached to the loft was broken in half and also lay on the floor in shambles. About the only thing left standing on the inside of the cabin was the rock solid stone fireplace. George walked in the front door and slowly looked around the room. He was hoping to find some sort of anything that would help his mind fall back into the bliss that was his life here four decades earlier. There were no signs of life in or around this structure, and Stone was finally starting to believe time had caught up to this wonderful home. There were no pictures, no cleaned rifles, and no signs that anyone cared for this cabin.

George looked around one last time and noticed one item that jumped out to him. It was the porcelain vase that used to sit on top of the table by the fire. It was the vase he had used to wash his hands and face. What made this so curious to George was that in this room and in this cabin of total destruction, this porcelain vase was unharmed. It was probably the most fragile item in the room, but it seemed to suffer little damage. It was easy for George Stone to see why it had not been destroyed. It was sitting in the middle of the solid stone fireplace. George stepped into the cabin and walked around the room, trying to avoid the large pieces of wood that could collapse even more if he were not careful. With every step he took, the floor gave a cracking sound as if each step would be his last. This cabin would have and probably should have fallen years ago if not for the solid walls. It was as if the cabin had one last gift for George and it had protected it all these years, waiting for his return.

George walked over to the fireplace, reached down, and grabbed the dusty old vase. It was brown with dust and covered in cobwebs. He picked it up and held it close, then started to wipe the dust clear of it. This once solid white vase was now a yellow color but still as strong as the day it came out of the kiln. George began to clean the dust off the vase then lifted it to his face and looked inside. To his surprise, there was a small envelope with a letter inside.

George took a step back and almost dropped the valued possession as he suddenly realized Eve must have thought he was alive. The letter had to be to him, but he was afraid to pull it out just in case he was wrong. He looked back to the door hoping to see someone standing there, but no one was. In his old age he had begun to wish for things he knew were never possible. It was his internal clock ticking. He looked back to the fireplace and as his old, red, vein-filled eyes rolled by the broken window, another sight caught them. Through the broken window he could see the Stone Chapel he and Eve built so many years ago. He quickly turned and walked out the front door and around the side of the cabin to the Chapel that was about thirty feet away from the cabin. The Stone Chapel had aged but was still standing strong. This was the true fruit of his labor. He stepped inside the simple gazebo and sat down on the stone seat that lined the wall. It was a seat he and Eve had shared many times. His old face began to wrinkle up, and he started to smile and cry at the same time. His blue eyes, still standing out strong in the sun, fought off the wrinkles that formed with the tears as he reached inside the vase and pulled out the letter. It had his name on it.

George was speechless as he softly set the vase down on the stone floor of his Stone Chapel and slowly examined the outside of the letter. He turned the dusty old sealed document over several times and rubbed his fingers along it. It was a precious gift, one he had not received in forty years. He wanted so badly to open it but could not because once he did he would no longer be able to enjoy the anticipation. He put the letter in his hand and pressed it against his cheek. He closed his eyes and he could see Eve sitting there with him. He was an old man, but she was not. Eve was still the young, beautiful woman he'd loved for so many years sitting across from him.

"Go ahead ... open it!" he heard her say in his mind. *"I wrote it for you!"* His eyes remained closed as her gentle English voice began to echo again in his brain. It was a sound that he had not heard in so long and for it to ring so true in his mind was special. George tried to imagine more as he kept his eyes closed and the letter pressed to his face.

"*I never forgot you, you know that, right? I love you, and I always will. I knew you were alive, and I knew you would return to me one day,*" he heard her say in his mind. Thoughts of her and her new family were starting to roll back into his head. So he opened his eyes and pulled the letter back down in front of him. He was now starting to openly weep so hard the tears were falling onto the letter. With no haste, he stuck his finger into the end of the letter and ripped the envelope open. He quickly pulled out the letter that seemed surprisingly long. It appeared to be two or three pages long. He took one last breath to try and control his emotions and then began to read her words that he had not seen in years.

George,

I love you and miss you more than you will ever know. First let me say I know that you are alive. I came back to this cabin this summer and noticed that a number of your things were missing. It broke my heart to look up and see the canister of letters gone. How could I have missed you? I did move back to Dover but tried to make it up here every month or two at least the first few years. After that it was twice a year. I knew you did not die, and I knew our love would never die. Why didn't you come find me? If you get this, please come find me. I'm living in Dover now, and I'm still waiting for you. I still wear your ring, and I have since that special day you put it on my finger. I even changed my name to Stone for you. I wait and I wait for your return, but you never came. Why didn't you come find me? Did you think I had died? I've remained close friends with the church since moving back to Dover. They've been so good to me over the years. I miss you so much. Where are you? I thought about trying to track you down in America, but I do not know where to start. What if your life has moved on without me? What if you have moved on? I don't think I could take that kind of rejection. So I wait for you to come home. I have one other surprise for you, and I wanted to tell you this when you were in the camp, but I didn't want you doing something that might have gotten you killed. I didn't want you to try to get out and be shot. George, I had your daughter shortly after the war ended. She was very sick and born extremely early with some medical conditions because I was apparently pregnant when I was shot. It was very early on, and I'm amazed we did not lose the child; you have a daughter. She is very small and will probably be her entire life, but she is very real and very special. She even knows all about her father, at least as much as I could tell her. Her name is "Wild Stone." Do you like it? I thought you would. I was able to give her the name of the two most important men in my life. Her middle name is Nada, after my mother. She hopes to someday see her father.

George was crying so hard that the tears began to fall on the paper and smear some of the words. He pulled the letter up higher so the paper was no longer at risk of getting wet, for he did not want to ruin any of it.

I have so much to tell you. Now that I know you will return, I will leave this letter for you. I will come back to this cabin once a month until I'm sure you no longer have the ability to make it back. I will pull weeds from the Stone Chapel, and I will make sure that "Wild" knows her American history. We will be waiting for you to come back to us. Please return soon.

Your forever love,

EVE

The letter was dated April 1954. The letter was safely protected in the vase in the cabin for thirty-two years. Over time Eve must have given up hope of his return and set the letter and the vase inside the fireplace for safe keeping just in case he ever made it back.

George sat in disbelief for minutes that turned into hours. He read and reread the letter more times than he could remember. It was like a really good song he played over and over in his head. But this was thirty-two years later. *What have I done? I had a chance so many years ago to talk to her but made the wrong decision. How could I ever live with myself now?* He thought. This woman waited for him, but something in the water and the pipes caused him to make a different decision. Something made him choose another path, and while it turned out to be a great path, this large walkway still existed, and he had never known it. The letter was thirty-two years old! Even the daughter he had never known would be close to forty years old now. George leaned over and put the letter back in the vase. He reached into his jacket pocket and pulled out a dried sunflower that he'd saved in a book for dozens of years and dropped it in the vase. He had no response as he put both of his hands over his face and began to weep out loud. It was the most intense cry of his life, but it was a cry only he heard. He cried from his heart, and he cried from his soul. He cried until he had no water left in his body to shed another tear. His old blue eyes were so swollen from the tears he could barely see to find his way back down the mountain.

After several hours sitting in the Stone Chapel, the dying man rose to his feet and picked up the vase. He also reached down and picked up a large rock. He walked back to the cabin, went inside, and worked his way back to the fireplace. He pulled the letter out of the vase, folded it in half, and stuck it in his jeans pocket. He grabbed the envelope from the letter and held it against the stone fireplace. He then pulled a small pencil out of his back jeans pocket. He took the pencil and wrote a few words that were only for Eve to see. He then placed it in the pit. He took the dried sunflower and put it down as well. He leaned down to his knees, put the rock on top of the envelope and the dried sunflower, then rose back to his feet. He held the vase tightly as his sore eyes looked around the cabin. This man did not have a lot of time left, and he did not know what to do. This day had been an emotional ride for him. He was more confused than he had ever been in his life. He was stunned, hurt, and shaken all at the same time, but the only thing he felt like doing was walking back down the mountain. So George turned and walked out the door, carrying the yellow vase. He stopped and took one last look at the Stone Chapel he'd loved so much. He took a big breath … then began walking straight back down the mountain, never looking back.

Now the only way I can truly love her is to never talk to her again, he thought. *I'll be dead soon, and it will just hurt them more. To them I must have died a long time ago. Apparently I did.*

George didn't realize it at the time, and he would never realize it the rest of his days … he was making the same mistake a second time. George Stone gave up.

Epilogue

The old woman stood overlooking her Stone Chapel Valley. She was holding a dried sunflower and a letter in one hand and her small metal woven ring in the other along with the blanket she had wrapped around her.

Every night for the rest of my life I will be wondering if he will ever write me back. Maybe he will send a letter in the mail ... something.

He does not. My love is complete and will never be approached again. It would be too difficult. The attrition of the soul has won. I have nothing left but everything else, she thought quietly.

Eve tossed the dried sunflower and letter out into the wind. They quickly caught the cold winter air and flew off into the distance. She reached down and pulled the old metal ring off her finger and dropped it to the ground. She turned her aged body back around and began walking back the way she came.

SUNFLOWERS
BY GEORGE STONE
1967 ELLIOTT AWARD WINNING ESSAY

I often wonder why a flower has to die so quickly. Why something so beautiful is allowed to live for such a short period of time and then it's gone. I wonder why we are given what we are given and then it's gone. The times we share and the lives we live are but a small petal on the flower that is life. Our time is so short. Our lifetime is so short, so how do we make a difference? How do we make sure that we matter? Why do we get up the next day? The answer is very simple ... like the flower; they are the special moments in our lives. They are the short times of highs and euphoria that get us through the day, the week, the year, and the lifetime. If we did not have these little successes, these little tastes of victory, then we would have no reason to live. If we were truly given what we thought we wanted, then we would have no reason, no goal, and no reward to search out.

In this life, our very short life, we are given the flower, and we are given the love, and we are given the need. That's why we go on. The special moments, no matter how short or how sweet, become our motivators. The moments will forever serve as the special rewards that we have earned. That is why the flower cannot live forever. That is why the love we share and the love we crave are so short. That is why the love we have we always seem to take for granted and long for more and for something more real. In life we have the perfect love, but too much of that love diminishes the craving for it. The craving is there and it's just as strong as it could ever be; yet we see it all the time. We feel it all the time, and we become resistant to it. It no longer becomes the reward; it becomes part of the journey.

The key is to realize that the flower will die, and it should be appreciated for what it was. It needs to be admired and remembered and truly loved, then let go to blossom forever in your mind. It will always remind you of the special things, the special times, the special places, and the special people. It's perfect, even in its death, because without the death, the flaws of the flower would eventually show and depreciate the value of it. That's how life is. The key is to remember the flower must die or inside we all will.

The key is to take the garden you are given and watch it grow. Water it, feed it, and from time to time walk around and look at it from another angle.

The garden we grow is the true reward. Make your garden grow and make it flourish with the colors of the world. Make it everything you want it to be, because that is why it exists. Too many people water their gardens and watch it grow and then pick it clean. They forget the seeds need to be replanted every year. My garden is a great one. I never know what's going to grow, but I continue to water it. Sometimes weeds will grow, but you just have to clean them out from time to time to keep the garden healthy and beautiful. Do this and your special favorite flower will grow in your garden, even if you've never planted the seed. It will grow, and it will be big and beautiful and will bloom as proudly as any flower that ever existed. Just remember—it will die as well, and that will be the motivator to work hard in your garden and grow another.

The special things in our lives keep us living, striving for more. These special things make us realize how special we are and how special our life is and can be. Right now there is a beautiful flower about to bloom, and no one will ever see it. But that won't stop it from becoming beautiful. That won't stop it from making a difference, and that won't stop it from dying. That is life; that is why we are.

Although watching the flower die is probably the hardest thing we will ever have to do, it's the flower's death that keeps us alive. Love is the life that runs through all of us; without it we are empty. Love is also like life. It changes sometimes to meet our needs sometimes because too much of anything will eventually tire.

George Stone, 1967

HIS ATTRITION

It seems to me; the scenery just flows by,
It seems to me, that no one even knows I've died.
It seems to me, the beauty in the life is gone,
It seems to me, the vision I had was so strong.
But now it's time to realize,
I'm not the man I've immortalized.
The time is gone and nothing here feels,
That pain that burns is oh so real ... and it seems to me, the beauty in her
    eyes was brief.
It seems to me, the soul she gave is now relief.
It seems to me, what we had was more than dreams.
It seems to me, I never wanted just the little things.
But now it's time to realize,
It's not the dream we immortalized.
The time is gone and nothing here feels,
The pain that burns is a soul with less appeal.
But now it's time to realize,
My father's days are in front of my eyes.
The life I've lived is now inside,
I can't bring it out, so alone it cries ... and.
It seems to me, memories are leaving mind,
It seems to me, the life I thought ... I'll never find.
It seems to me, the wind that blows is blowing us,
It seems to me, my face collects other's dust.
It seems to me, life is defined by more than that,
It seems to me, it only hurts if I look back.
George Stone, 1986

GEORGE STONE

Had he not been so trustworthy and loyal, he probably would have never signed up for the army at such a young age. But George Alexander Stone knew there was more to life then the little town of White City, Kansas. This was the place he was born and where he hoped to return to someday to build his own farm. His family had lived here as long as he could remember. Each generation would build on the last and farm the land.

While he had several uncles, aunts, and cousins, his immediate family was a much smaller group. His father, Warren, spent his days in the field while his mother did her part around the farm. In fact, she was the magic ingredient that made the food grow. His sister, Elizabeth, had turned into a fine young woman, but his other brother had died several years earlier. So when George decided to enlist in the army, his family was proud but devastated at the same time. This group had come to depend on the young, five-foot-ten, brown haired, blue-eyed soldier as a fighter of their own, and now he was leaving.

All he knew was he would be the first to leave this small town. His smile was electric to everyone who saw it, and the thought of losing that at a time of war weighed heavy on his family. George was one of the smartest kids in his high school and had actually made it to his senior year. This was a great accomplishment, as most kids his age had already dropped out to work their farms. George always found it amusing that he was considered the one who would leave, when all he really wanted to do was see the world and then come home. That is why he enlisted. He was not concerned about the war, and he was not concerned about the draft; he just wanted to see the world for what it was ... real, not just pictures in a book. George Stone walked with a slight limp, and while he never really knew why he had the limp, he felt it was his job to earn it. He'd spent many summer nights dreaming about the world outside Kansas, and now he was about to get his opportunity to live out those dreams—at least as much as the army would let him.

George Stone was from a small town but would have to grow up in a very short period time. He was sent off to war when he was very young. This would change his life forever. In the world that had become so violent and so disenchanted, he would find something to fight for. George would end up in the most dangerous place in the world yet somehow manage to find true paradise. It was a war and a life he had never envisioned, but it was one he was not about to live the rest of his life without. In this place, life could end in just a matter of seconds. While this would keep him on the edge, the life he would discover would bring him back.

EVE WILD

Eve Wild was a twenty-year-old country girl from England who was forced to live on her own in a place of quiet solitude. Her life had been much more simple a couple of years before in Dover, England. She wasn't a line over five-foot-five and usually kept her hair flat enough to stay under that line. Her eyes were a light shade of green, and her father used to tell her that's because she was born in the hills surrounded by the green forest. While this was a great tale, she never believed him. The young woman loved her mother, Nada, and her father, Richard, although most around her town didn't.

Her father was a lawman of sorts, a constable, as called in these parts, and he'd made many enemies, but Eve could never understand why. To her, Richard was more than a father; he was her best friend. To this point in her life, she was an only child, and her father treated her like a daughter and a son. He taught her how to read. He also taught her how to survive. Both were strong qualities that would stay with her forever. She never liked to wear a dress, as she just did not feel comfortable in the fabric. She preferred to spend most of her days working around the homestead in her worn-out overalls. Eve used small pins to hold them up because she felt more freedom in the loose-fitting clothes. Being an only child and unmarried entering her twenties was pretty rare in those days. It was the fear of her father and her home-style dress that kept most town boys away.

But Eve would be robbed of her youth. She would be forced to put her father's teachings to good use. But out of the tragedy that would befall her, Eve would also be rewarded with the love of a good man. Her time and her place would collide with his, and he would become the love of her life. But it was a short love and a love she would spend the rest of her life holding on to. All Eve wanted was the accounting of the day, and she needed a reason to go on fighting for the world she had long since lost. There was only one other man who could replace the love and respect she had known in her father. When he was taken away, Eve would be sent spinning into a world of unknown, a world of danger. This was a place where Eve had truly found herself, but it was this man who would find her and would completely change her world.

RICHARD WILD

Richard Wild was an English lawman that only wanted peace and safety for his family and town. He never wanted to wear the badge, but it was forced upon him. He took the title in stride and protected everything the English law stood for as long as it meant justice. Richard did what he had to do. This was his way, but it was not the way of some who shared his blood. Richard Wild was caught between what he knew he had to do and what the actual results would be if he did it. It was the law of the land in 1930s England. It was not the American old west but rather a later version of it. The stories of the American outlaw legend made its way across the Atlantic, and these were now the men Wild would deal with on a daily basis. Wild feared nothing. Righteousness was his biggest trait; righteousness was also his biggest downfall. Always having to be right and good had a downside, as Wild would soon discover. He had a wife, a daughter, and a homestead that all would be jeopardized by his righteousness ... his intimidation ... his condemnation. Wild's family tree had several wild and untrimmed branches.

This is the story of three people all living in a dangerous place at a dangerous time. One would die for the cause, the other two would fall in love fighting for theirs. But how long would they be willing to battle the war of attrition and time? It is a war few can win because it takes too much from the soul to beat it. This is their story. This is their attrition, and this is their wearing of their souls.

The Author and the Story

Alan Shope is currently a TV sports reporter working in Wichita, Kansas, at the ABC affiliate KAKE.

My Attrition is Mr. Shope's second novel. His first, *A Different Heaven*, was published in 2005 and can be ordered at any major bookstore. Alan Shope has been working in TV news for eighteen years. As a reporter, Alan has won dozens of awards and was twice nominated for an Emmy. In his spare time, he has written hundreds of short stories, as well as six movie manuscripts, and worked on a variety of other projects. He has also written and recorded twenty-three original music scores and currently owns a U. S. patent and trademark.

FROM THE AUTHOR

The story of *My Attrition* was inspired by actual letters, notes, and events exchanged by two lifelong friends whose names will not be mentioned but will forever be remembered. Although the letters have been slightly altered for the purposes of this story, the content remains accurate. *My Attrition* is the wearing effect that we all feel from time to time, but when it wears on the soul it must be addressed and discussed or it will sit in the gut forever. If you have something to get off your chest, do it now or regret it forever. That is the reason for *My Attrition*. Everyone has a really long, sad letter to write, and this one is mine.

A college professor once learned he had cancer and had a short time to live. That evening he asked his class to list one hundred different things they wanted to do in their lives. His last request for the class was to complete that list over their lifetime. I never knew him for anything more than his last name, which to this day slips my mind. He died a short time later. I was in that college class nearly seventeen years ago, and I'm happy to say there are only eleven items left on my list. The professor would be proud. The inspiration for this book was number sixty-four on that list. The numbers did not have any significance. However, had it not been for number sixty-four, the letters in this book would have never been discovered, and this story would live only in memory. I guess it's time I go bungee jump … number sixty-eight.

Please send thoughts, comments, or questions about
My Attrition **to:** ashope@kake.com.

Printed in the United States
144372LV00005B/1/P

9 780595 532322